B·E·R·Y·L

Food and Friends

B·E·R·Y·L
Food and Friends

BERYL REID

with the assistance of	and many talented gastronome,	Drawings by
Eric Braun	**William Chappell**	**Ian Ribbons**

Foreword by
SIR HARRY SECOMBE CBE

EBURY PRESS · LONDON

Published by Ebury Press
Division of The National Magazine Company Ltd
Colquhoun House
27–37 Broadwick Street
London W1V 1FR

First impression 1987

ISBN 0 85223 662 X

Editor: Suzanne Webber
Art Director: Frank Phillips
Designer: Bill Mason
Picture Research: Jan Croot
Filmset and printed by BAS Printers Limited,
Over Wallop, Hants
Bound by Butler and Tanner Ltd,
Frome, Somerset

Contents

Acknowledgements

*R*ecipes are among the most difficult things in the world to trace back to their precise origins and the best I can do in this book is to acknowledge with thanks the people who have helped us to track down half-remembered combinations of ingredients and the books which have been my inspiration through so many happy years at Honeypot Cottage, both in and out of the kitchen.

Since its publication in 1958 my cooking Bible has been Elizabeth Campbell's *Encyclopedia of World Cookery*, published by Spring Books for Paul Hamlyn for thirty bob (£1.50) and now worth its weight in gold, if you can beg, borrow or steal a copy. Recipes from Australia to Yugoslavia are all there – and so easy to follow I'd recommend them to any beginner or anyone who just loves cooking.

Shirley Sutton and her sister Sandra researched for us a rare old English recipe from Elizabeth Ayrton's *English Provincial Cooking*, published by Mitchell Beazley; while another delicacy, Poor Knights of Windsor was tracked down in Kathie Webber's *International Star Cook Book*, published by the TV Times. Iain Gordon, quick as a flash, unearthed from the *Glasgow Cookery Book*, issued by the Glasgow and West of Scotland College of Domestic Science, the way to make my favourite Queen of Puddings, cooked by my mother when I was very young.

Another of my Very Young Favourite Things was A.A. Milne's book *Now We Are Six*, published by Methuen in 1927, from which I recalled the little poem about King John, but for the last word on our 'local' King I turned to Maurice Ashley's *Life and Times of King John* (Weidenfeld and Nicholson).

Warm thanks again to all friends who have provided help and recipes in the text and I must record my special affection and gratitude to my dear friend Harry Secombe, a pal for so many years, for the loving Foreword he has contributed to this book. God bless the autobiography he's now writing – and in long-hand, the plucky lad!

Dedication

To everyone who loves food

As the Italians so charmingly put it,
'May your shadow never grow less...'

Foreword

*A*nyone passing a certain 'Honeypot Cottage' at night time might, until recently, have been surprised by a seductive female voice calling from the back door, 'Come on in Sir Harry, it's bed time' and other similar blandishments. However, things were not as salacious as they seemed to be – it was not Miss Beryl Reid OBE tempting me into her boudoir, she was merely trying to seduce one of her many cats to come in. Unfortunately Sir Harry, the runt of the litter, has now passed away, the burden of knighthood perhaps being too much for him. I was saddened at the news because I had been inordinately 'chuffed' at having a cat called after me – the ultimate accolade.

It was typical of Beryl's generosity to name one of her cats in this way. She has been a dear friend of mine since the early Fifties when we appeared together in 'Educating Archie', then at the Palladium, and on many occasions since then on TV and the stage. We had lots of laughs together, and the story she tells of the time we shared lobster and caviar on the fire escape at the Palladium I remember with particular affection.

Beryl is one of that very select band of performers who have successfully crossed that perilous bridge from the variety stage to the more prestigious legitimate side of the profession. To be able to play the Palladium and the National Theatre with equal success is every actor's dream.

She can be hysterically funny – who can forget her Spanish maid impression – and she can be incredibly moving, as she was as Alec Guinness's ex-girlfriend in 'Tinker, Tailor, Soldier Spy'. There are many facets to this talented lady's character, but they all add up to one indomitable, endearing person of whom I am very very fond.

Harry Secombe

1
Childhood
and Early Eating

I never thought it could be so wonderful. I never thought I could enjoy it so much and find it so exciting, or that it would give me so much pleasure to please other people. Cooking, I'm talking about; because, you see, when I was little and living in my mother and father's house, my mother never let me go into the kitchen. She used to say, 'Away you go, Beryl – you're just a nuisance.' She was a very good, plain Scottish cook, who used to present me every day of my young life with two puddings, in case there was one that I didn't like but never gave me the opportunity to see how she worked. I never knew how she did *anything*, so when she said to me one day when she was not very well, 'Will you put some water in the teapot, Beryl,' of course I put cold water in, because I didn't know you had to put boiling water in: nobody was more ignorant about *everything* in the kitchen than I was.

When I was sixteen and a half and had decided to go on the stage and had got my first show in Bridlington, at £2 a week, I said to my mother, 'Mummy, when I go on the stage what mustn't I eat?' I thought she was going to give me a long list of things that I had to avoid but she said, 'Well, soap or rusty nails', which of course wasn't what I expected at all. So that is how I set off on my career, not only as a performer and actress, but also as a non-cooking person.

THE BIG BLACK POT

I can remember that, when I was at home, my mother always had a great big black saucepan – very old-fashioned, of course, I suppose – but it was the stock-pot and it was always going. She used to buy marrow bones and every vegetable that you could imagine, and just used to add them all to the pot and boil it up again, so that we always had soup first – 'Soup of the evening, beautiful soup' as Alice in Wonderland's Gryphon (or was it the Mock Turtle?) used to enthuse. My mother's soup was strictly a winter treat. She'd never heard about anything like cold soup in the summer, but I hadn't either.

In the pantry in the kitchen there used to be a marble slab on which she put the big black pot to cool down, then any fat that had formed was taken off and some more vegetables were put in for the next day. This soup was something that I'm sure kept us very healthy when we were very little – as did porridge, of course, but porridge with salt on. Nobody in our family, because it was a Scottish family, had ever heard of sugar going on porridge, even less golden syrup, which used to be a treat that took the curse off breakfast-time for people in the army later, when the war was on. You could have milk on the porridge but you had to have salt. The porridge used to be made in a double saucepan and was quite a performance. This soup and porridge were the things that were considered very nutritious and, I'm sure, did my brother and myself a great deal of good.

MY BEST PUDDING

Mummy made lovely puddings, like **Queen of Puddings**, with meringue on top, or imaginative things like a peach in the bottom of a little dish, with egg custard set on top. When it was turned out you laughed, because it looked like a poached egg. Since those days I have learnt how to make **Queen of Puddings**, and here's the recipe:

Queen of Puddings *The ingredients are: ½ pint milk; 1 oz butter; 2 oz breadcrumbs; 2 eggs; grated rind of 1 lemon; 1 oz sugar plus 2 tablespoons; 2–3 tablespoons jam.*

Heat the milk with the butter to boiling point then pour it over the breadcrumbs. Let it soak for a few minutes, then add the yolks of the eggs, the grated lemon rind and 1 oz sugar. Mix all these together, pour into a pie dish and bake at Gas Mark 4/350°F/ 180°C until set. Take out of the oven, spread jam over it and allow to cool slightly. Whisk the egg whites until very stiff. Fold in 2 tablespoons sugar. Spread over the top of the pudding. Return to the oven and bake until the meringue is a very pale brown.

This was what I thought of as my Best Pudding; you see, we didn't have a great number of sweet things at all. Oh, it was something special! In those days all I could gather was that it appeared to have a sponge-type base and then there was strawberry jam – real strawberry jam, of course – and then there was meringue. My mother didn't have a mixer on which you turned the handle, or any of those convenient things to beat up egg whites and sugar; she used to have the egg whites on a flat plate with the sugar and she'd beat them – sort of swish them round on the flat plate with a silver knife – until the sugar and the egg white began to look like a meringue mixture, all stiff and ready to go on the concoction underneath. Of course, everything was extremely hard work in those days – there were no easy ways or short cuts.

BLOTTED FISH

Mother used to cook lovely fish, but everything that had to be fried was 'blotted'. By 'blotting' I mean that she used to put the fried fish onto the kitchen paper equivalent which was in fact the creamy absorbent paper, which fishmongers always put round the fish and in which fish and chips are always wrapped these days. If she ever roasted potatoes, they had to be 'blotted' too. I didn't really know how she did it, but at least we weren't eating any fat.

SMELLY LENA AND SCHOOLGIRL'S KNICKERS

When I went to school I used to have school dinners and little did I know what effect they would have on my future career. If we had what we called 'Smelly Lena' which, of course, was semolina or tapioca, it used to go straight into my handkerchief and up my knickers, then into the nearest loo I could find – that was the treatment for anything I didn't like and as I had those navy blue, fleecy-lined knickers, it never seemed to matter very much, as long as they were washed often enough! Here I was storing up material for later on, when I was to do a character called Monica in 'Educating Archie', She was the St. Trinian's-type school-girl who used to store up everything in her knickers until it grew penicillin. Fortunately, in my schooldays nothing stayed up there long enough to germinate. I can always remember at eleven o'clock in the morning we used to be given hot milk (I was now about six and getting grown-up). There was a boy called Freddie Walton whom I took a terrible dislike to; I really bordered on hating him because he used to let the skin settle on the top of his hot milk and then eat the skin before he drank the milk and I thought he was 'absolutely dishgushting!' as Monica would have said.

'Absolutely dishgushting!'

I can't remember very well the meat we used to eat at school except that I did develop an absolute loathing for rabbit. To this day, although I cook it for my cats now, and it's really quite expensive, there's something about the shape of it and the smell of it and the handling of it that still quite upsets me. The meat was usually ordinary meat and never very much of it, like very thinly cut lamb, or chicken, which, of course tasted so wonderful then. I think something terrible has happened to battery-reared chickens these days – but I remember they used to be such a treat. If we had a chicken at home it was a special morning, and we rejoiced because it was going to be chicken for Sunday lunch. We almost always had mashed potato – more crumbly than creamy, actually – never, never chips or crisps or those sorts of things, which seem to be a great speciality in school dinners now.

At school we used to have things like poached eggs: the food was always very plain, and again, funnily enough, there was never any fat attached to it. Obviously people thought then that fat was very bad for you, and I think now that they were absolutely right. When I see some of the school dinners today on television, or hear about them from parents, they're all the worst things for spotty children: chips or crisps and virtually no meat at all except perhaps a little mince. Cabbage was another thing we used to have, which tasted and looked watery. The trick then, I think, was to boil it within an inch of its life. I can make cabbage taste much better nowadays but, on the other hand, I can't eat cabbage cooked as people sometimes cook it now, when it's hardly seen the water. I don't like vegetables that are too crunchy, like cauliflower, and I can't bear the smell of it cooking: it reminds me of schoolgirls' knickers being washed.

Our fare then, was very very plain, but I suppose, as we were all absolutely all right, it was very very good for us. After school I used to go home and have a sort of 'knife and fork tea', as they would call it in Scotland. We didn't have dinner in the evening at home, but 'something rather nice for tea'; perhaps a bit of fish, like haddock cooked in milk with a little bit of butter. We always ate very delicate things.

Roasted Chicken *Sprinkle salt over the skin of the chicken and rub it in. Then prick the skin as if it were something you'd taken an instant dislike to. Fill it with some stuffing which my mother used to make, as I do now, with egg, breadcrumbs (she used to make the bread hard in the oven and put it through the mincer but I use the whizzer), mixed dried herbs, salt and pepper. I tart it up a bit now by putting in a bit of lemon juice. If it's too dry, add a little milk and maybe put a bit of garlic at the end of the chicken and a slice of lemon, because the chickens don't taste as exciting as they did then. Then roast the chicken according to size – ours would be quite a 'bonny bird' – at Gas Mark 7/425°F/220°C for 15 minutes, then turn down to Gas Mark 4/350°F/180°C for the rest of the time. The chicken is done if, when you prick the thickest part of a leg with a fork, the juices run clear. With the chicken we would always have roast potatoes ('blotted', of course) and my brother Roy would always have the parson's nose – that was absolutely nothing to do with me as he was the eldest.*

Another of my mother's recipes that I loved and was only told how to make when I was grown up was called **Potted Meat,**

Potted Meat *For four people, take 1½ lb shin of beef or best stewing steak with the fat cut off. Cut the beef into small chunks. Put into a saucepan with about 1½ pints of water. Season with salt and pepper and a good pinch of blade mace. My mother used to use a cow heel but you can't get those now, so I use 2 pig's trotters. Cook the whole lot in a pressure cooker for 1 hour or simmer in an ordinary saucepan for 2½–3 hours. While it's cooking keep checking that the water hasn't boiled away. Remove the trotters, taking care to remove all the small bones – these you can eat yourself if you like them. Drain off the stock, setting it aside and put the meat through the mincer or food processor. Put it into a pie dish and pour over the remaining liquid (about ½ pint) to moisten and let it cool, then put it in the fridge to set. Lovely with English mustard, and beetroot with vinegar or redcurrant jelly.*

MUMMY AND THE JELLY

When I was small I didn't have many parties and when we did have parties we had jelly. If I got wind that my mother was making a jelly I used to go out and shout, 'We're having a *party* – Mummy's making a *jelly*!' and she would be all red in the face and try to get me to come in. I was allowed to have children to little parties on my birthday, but I was absolutely not allowed to say that it was my birthday, so we had the awful experience of having a few children there and making up games and things but not saying that it was my birthday, because my mother said that would be

'My girlfriend's not for sharing.' Susannah York, myself and Coral Browne in 'The Killing of Sister George'.

like asking for a present. So any fancy ideas about birthdays were knocked on the head – in fact I never had a birthday cake until I was doing the filming in London of 'The Killing of Sister George'. I suddenly thought of never having had a birthday cake and I think I must have mentioned it to a lot of people, so I got seven birthday cakes!

SPRING MEDICINE AT AYR

One of the most marvellous things about being very young was having a little farm cottage eight miles out of Ayr in Scotland and two miles from a tiny fishing village called Dunure. In fact we had it practically all through our schooldays. Of course, as the herring boats used to come into this toy-sized harbour we children used to go and meet them at four o'clock in the morning. It was quite an adventure: as the boats sailed in, we were waiting there with baskets as big as we could carry. The fishermen used to shout, 'Come along, children: herrings ha'pennies each – ha'pennies each!', so we had to fill up our baskets and carry home as many herrings as we could for 'ha'pennies each'.

When we got them back we used to eat them ravenously: my mother and Auntie Belle used to clean and gut them, roll them in oatmeal and grill them. Sometimes we had mustard sauce, which I thought was absolutely lovely, though it was considered a bit rich for children. Those herrings were beautiful – I mean, I don't think I've ever tasted anything so lovely. You know how tastes stay with you and you can often remember incidents very clearly by a taste or a smell. The herrings were one of the wonderful things about staying at Dunure; the other wonderful thing was that we used to get an enormous boiling fowl for half a crown (about $12\frac{1}{2}$p) from the farm where everything was so inexpensive. I remember that Auntie Belle would stand in the stream behind the cottage and tuck her frock in her knickers, and pluck and clean this boiling fowl. I learned to pluck one, from watching her, because it's so much easier to learn from watching people. Once plucked, it used to be put in an enormous pot with all the vegetables we could also collect locally. There really were no shops – a butcher's van would call twice a week, and we used to have some meat from that, though I can't remember it terribly well. Sausages were called links and they were a butcher's treat. I loved them. Of course we used to have the potted meat I told you about.

On other occasions, rather festive occasions, we used to have **Special Boiling Fowl** (hopefully for half a crown!):

Special Boiling Fowl

Cut the chicken into joints. Put all the pieces into a pan and cover with a little salt. Add a small skinned onion, bring to the boil and simmer for about 2 hours. The time will vary, according to the age and size of the bird. Take out the pieces of chicken and take the skin off, because a great deal of fat lurks in chicken skin. Arrange them on a dish and keep them warm. Then prepare the sauce, by making a roux of 2 oz flour and 2 oz butter. Gradually add ½ pint of the chicken stock. Bring this to the boil, stirring all the time, so that it is smooth and thick. Take off the heat and add the yolk of 1 egg, 1 teaspoon of lemon juice and ½ pint cream (which, of course, was also very cheap from the farm) which have all been blended together. Reheat the sauce, without boiling it, pour it over the fowl and serve.

These, of course, were the most carefree days of my life and a sort of ideal way for children to live. We played all day, and we didn't have to dress up – it was all marvellous. The only thing that seemed like a faint cloud on the horizon, was that my brother, who was four years older than me, always had what was called a 'holiday task.' His holiday task one year was to read Milton's 'Paradise Lost', and as we'd had such a lovely six or eight weeks or whatever it was, he started to read it the night before we were coming home, so I don't actually think he put his heart into it. I don't know quite how he managed when he was questioned about the Downfall of Satan, but he was very bright anyhow – much brighter than me.

One of the glorious things about being there was that Auntie Belle had a wonderful way of making Lemonade. She used cream of tartar, fresh lemons, hot water and lump sugar. This we used to drink by the gallon and plead her to keep making it for us. But the thing we didn't care for so much was called Spring Medicine, for which I've found the recipe: 1 oz cream of tartar, as in the first recipe (it all starts very nicely again) BUT 1 oz Epsom salts, 1 lemon cut into slices, lump (loaf) sugar to taste, 2 pints, or less, of boiling water poured over. This was something we *weren't* quite so keen on!

2
Poverty Row: Baked Beans and After

When I had grown up a bit and was really getting on, I thought, with my stage career, I got one or two touring dates, among them a little show called 'Blue Skies'. In those days I shared what they called a 'combined room', with three beds, with a girl called Anita Eaton, who later married the 'I Lift Up My Finger and I Say Tweet Tweet' singer-comedian Leslie Sarony, and Olivia Jevons, a dancer in the show, who is still one of my great friends.

We were terribly poor: we'd say, 'What shall we have today?' and somebody would look at the ceiling and say, 'Why don't we have some Baked Beans?', because they cost so little money, and they really did fill us up. It became almost a running gag with us: if we did happen to have a pause in the conversation, Baked Beans usually happened to crop up. I ate so many of them that, however lovely so many people seem to think them now, I am no longer really very tempted to eat them, because they practically came out of my ears. We thought of re-naming the show 'Blue Skies and Baked Beans'.

By Thursday in those days on Poverty Row we were quite flat broke: I remember Olivia's mother and my mother came to visit us and we were so ashamed because we had absolutely nothing to eat, because we were what was called 'self-catering' and we got paid on Friday. Between us we had the rind of a bit of gorgonzola cheese. Both the mothers were absolutely appalled that this was the way that we were living. We didn't seem to care at all: we thought that it was lovely being 'actresses' on the stage at St. Helen's, doing that Monday matinée for the miners, whose so evident 'couldn't care less' attitude and glum faces really brought you down to earth.

Of course, in the early days, potatoes seemed to play a great part in my staple diet. 'Self-catering' meant that you used to buy the food and ask the landlady to cook it: you just paid for the room and not even the heat, Landladies were mostly very good-hearted; I'm sure they threw a few bits in for us, because we really were pretty poverty-stricken. I remember one day we bought a lot of potatoes (we knew those filled you up) and I think we ran to a sausage each. I was the spokeswoman or spokesperson who was sent to deliver the potatoes to the landlady. 'We want these potatoes, please', I said. 'Boil them, but don't mash them!' I also handed over our precious meat ration of the three sausages. She looked at me rather aghast. What I meant, but could not explain to her, was that I wanted the same number of potatoes back that I'd given her, because we'd had to buy them and we were counting them.

When I did my first season at Bridlington, where I was in digs for twenty-five shillings a week (£1.25 – new money) which paid for Full Board, I really wasn't all that interested in food. I ate because I was hungry; the same thing in Scarborough, which was my next summer season – food was presented to me and I ate it because it was time to eat and also because it was necessary to exist, but my main interest then was in getting to the theatre.

THE SOUP KETTLE

I made the most terrible mistakes when I first started ever trying to cook anything. I had what was called a bed-sitter in Mornington Crescent that was so small you could hardly turn round in it, and my only cooking utensil was a kettle. Somebody told me, 'You can heat soup in a kettle, you know', so I did what I thought they meant, which was to pour a tin of soup into a kettle. The next time we were speaking I said, 'Yes, I did use the kettle for the soup but isn't it hard to get it out?!' I hadn't realized that they had meant me to open the tin, put it in the kettle then lift it out with something, and heat the soup in that way!

Early in my London days I was allowed to stay in somebody's flat. They had a frying pan and had left me bacon and eggs. I thought that was pretty swank – 'really Living', in fact, as Marlene of the Midlands would have put it. I lit the gas, turned it up as high as I could, put a frying pan on it, threw in the bacon and beat a hasty retreat to the other side of the room, because, of course, the fat was flying in every direction: my arms were burnt, the front of my legs were burnt – the fat was in my hair and narrowly missed my eyes. I wrote to my friends saying, 'Dear Julie and Arthur, I have cooked some bacon today, and doesn't it hurt!' My ignorance on the matter was total. Julie and Arthur were a wonderful act: Arthur Prince – star ventriloquist, with his figure Jim, and Julie, his wife and assistant. Arthur dressed as a ship's commander and Jim was a tiny little cabin boy. He also had an enormous figure called Monty which was the same size as himself. He used to have long conversations with Monty (which consisted more of listening to Monty's quips than having much to say himself) as they pretended to walk round the poop deck together. Julie and Arthur were very good to me – terribly kind, and always put me up if I had nowhere to stay.

BLUE NILE

This was the beginning of the war time, when I was hell bent on getting into ENSA. So I went to Drury Lane Theatre where the auditions were held by Basil Dean. The actors used to sing an irreverent song about him which I've always thought very funny indeed, so I make no apology for repeating it, although I did use it in my autobiography *So Much Love*. The ditty went like this:

> Basil, Basil, give us your ENSA, do;
> We're all crazy to do a show for you.
> According to Walter Hackett
> The thing's a bloody racket –
> But we'll look fine, standing twelve in a line
> On a stage that was built for two!

I did get in and joined the others living in hostels when we did the shows for ENSA. You were given your rations for the week and you had difficulty keeping them as actors are terrible and have absolutely no conscience where food is concerned. They always eat as if it's the last meal they're ever going to have and if you didn't get down very early in the morning for breakfast, all your rations would be swiped and you'd be left with absolutely nothing.

Food was, of course, terribly hard to come by and we all used to get extremely over-excited if we went to play an American base, because we knew that there we would have the chance of having a piece of steak. Can you imagine – *Steak*! Once when we went to a U.S. base these naughty American boys had made something called a Blue Nile cocktail (I have no idea at all of what went in it – I really didn't drink at all at that time) but it was a pretty foul taste. I thought I was being terribly grown-up and sophisticated – 'Oh, yes, thank you, I'll have another' – and it was the only time I've ever been properly drunk in my life. I wasn't the only one, because apparently the truck in which we were being driven back to our digs went over a hedge and I remembered nothing until I woke up next morning with a huge lump on my head. I've never had such a headache or been so sick; in fact it was an awfully good cure, and I make no apology for not giving a recipe for Blue Nile cocktail, except to advise that if you stumble across one – avoid it and run in the opposite direction!

ENTERTAINING GENTLEMEN

The Blue Nile cocktail was one kind of shock treatment – the most severe I received during my three years with ENSA, which were interspersed with other work, including touring variety shows. One of these was with Will Fyffe; Arthur and Julie Prince, who were so supportive to me in what I suppose have to be called my salad days – green salad, of course – were on the bill. A shock of another kind was in store on one of our weekly train calls on a Sunday. We had reserved compartments for however many people were travelling with the company – no loos, mind you, but reserved compartments. As I was the only girl in the show apart from the Dagenham Girl Pipers (who were rather closely guarded, I think) I was the one who was expected to find some food for the men to eat on the train. They always played cards all the time, and either lost their money or won some. During the week I had to go round wooing all the butchers to see if I could awaken a glimmer in anybody's eye. One week I found a butcher who really had quite a crush on me – pressed a bit of liver in my hand, and things like that – and by the end of the week I said to him, 'We really have nothing to eat on the train,' and I was limping a bit at the time (acting, of course!), so I was presented with an enormous pork pie. 'How marvellous,' I thought. 'They'll all be so thrilled with me'. I got in with all the card-playing gents. I had a paper plate and I also had a knife in my handbag – not to do anything evil with, but to cut up any food if I got any. They were playing cards; they weren't looking and I was just cutting the pie into pieces and pushing it into their hands as they went on with their game – then I looked at my bit and found it covered in thick black mould. They'd all eaten theirs, so I thought I'm going to get rid of mine; I put it under the seat, sort of rolled in the paper plate, and waited for them all to die. As they didn't know what they had eaten, and it was probably full of penicillin anyway, they didn't die on me, so that was one of my great escapes, really. This, perhaps, was what could be called my first attempt at 'entertaining gentlemen'. I do rather better now.

*One of my favourite
characters in the theatre – Gracie Fields.*

THEATRICAL LANDLADIES

I must say thinking back on it, that in those days during the war, landladies, were extremely creative and seemed to find little bits and pieces that I realize now were very inventive. This happened much more so in the North than in the South. One thing I can always remember the taste of was a really gorgeous cheese and onion pie with a pastry base. It was marvellous. It must have been made from a bit of old cheese and a few onions, which were not too diffiuclt to get hold of.

I remember arriving at one lot of digs and the landlady saying, 'Do you like fish and chips?' 'Er – yes,' I replied. 'Good,' she said, 'Because that's all you'll be getting!' There it was – every meal, at lunchtime as well as after the show. So I had to get to like fish and chips. I still do, actually. The wartime fish and chips from the shops were always wrapped in newspaper, which had a particular message for lots of people. I must say I loved them in newspaper, even eating them before I got home, with salt and vinegar from a big shaker in the shop.

I know that Gracie Fields adored fish and chips from her days in her home town of Rochdale; when she came back and they weren't wrapped in newspaper any longer she said, 'Oh, I don't like them any more – I don't fancy them now they're not wrapped in newspaper – it's just not the same!' Much later in her career when she returned from Capri to sing at the Batley Club in Yorkshire she found that their speciality was serving scampi and chips in a basket during the show. On the opening night she said, 'I know I was born over a fish and chip shop, but I never thought I'd be singing for my supper in one!'

By this time I was beginning to realize I was rather ambitious to do well on the stage. I always wanted, and in fact, still do, to do the best things, or better things, all the time. Discovering from the *Stage* newspaper that Tom Arnold was a great impresario in pantomime I thought, 'That's really what I've got to do – get a job with Tom Arnold.'

My mother actually came to London with me and we went to Brixton – I was, after all, extremely young still, though it's difficult to imagine now, when I see my face in the mirror in the morning and think 'There's a disaster area' – but less of that. We'd found these lovely people who were advertising in the *Stage* that they had digs to let, called Signor and Signora Pellegra. They had two daughters and I had a room in their house for ten shillings a week. They were extremely big-hearted people in every way: when Mussolini in his 'good days' for Italy had pleaded for money to help build roads

they sent their gold wedding rings and got tin ones back in return. As far as I was concerned, their generosity and helpfulness knew no bounds during the long weary days of walking from Brixton to Tom Arnold's office in Shaftesbury Avenue – a long hike that I doubt very much whether I could do today.

I have told in my first book how I got the job with Tom Arnold after three weeks of walking to an from Brixton and my temporary home with the Pellegras. God's a Funny Fellow; my persistence was rewarded by working for nine years in Tom Arnold pantomimes. During my lunch breaks from waiting in his outer office I used to go along to the Express Dairy. I had money for a cup of coffee, but not, perhaps, a bun or even Baked Beans, and I used to hope I'd meet someone I knew rich enough to treat me. I was usually very lucky and found somebody who'd say, 'Oh, hello, Beryl', which is always a good start for me. When I eventually did get the job I really had no way of knowing how to celebrate: At that young age of twenty-one I had not thought of just popping into a pub – I really didn't drink anyway except for the Guinness I was given in Blackpool for a special treat when I was sixteen-and-a-half (Ugh!) I draw a veil over the experience of the Blue Nile cocktails.

When I got the break, I thought, 'However can I celebrate this great achievement – Tom Arnold has given me a job – how can I think of something absolutely marvellous to have in way of celebration?' Eventually I went over the top – waving aside the waitress who'd grown so accustomed to my face over the past three weeks. When she said, 'Baked beans, Beryl?', I replied, with starry assurance, 'No, Grace; I'll have a double banana split!' Like most things in my life, when I remember them so clearly, I do find a recipe for them. But before I wallow in this celebratory nostalgia, I want to pay tribute to the wonderful thing that kept me going during this testing period, and that was the incredible kindness of my hosts in Brixton, The Pellegra family.

Although I was paying only ten shillings a week for my room, every evening when I got home they always offered to share their supper with me, which of course was spaghetti or pasta in one form or another. I could never erase them from my heart, because in those days it was that kind of thing that kept you alive. They had such a variety of lovely pasta dishes that I could fill a chapter with them, and though my interest at the time was mainly to eat to keep up my strength for my daily marathon, I have since learned how they did them and offer here one of the simplest and most economical:

Spaghetti with Oil and Garlic
(or tagliatelli, vermicelli, pasta shells)

The ingredients are: 12 oz spaghetti; 2 tablespoons oil; 1 garlic clove; 4 oz Parmesan cheese (from a sprinkler, if the real thing is not available for grating); parsley; salt and pepper.

Cook the pasta in a large pan of boiling salted water – if it's long spaghetti, feed it into the water until the immersed parts soften, then gently push the rest in. When soft but al dente *pour into a sieve or collander to drain. Put into a pan with the warmed oil and chopped garlic. Season with chopped parsley (preferably fresh parsley, which any fishmonger will give you if your're making a purchase). Serve with the grated cheese.*

After this nourishing Italian fare, here is the way to make the **Banana Split** which so gladdened my life in the West End back in 1941:

Banana Split

Peel 2 bananas and slice them lengthways down the middle. Arrange flat side up on a plate. Spoon 4 scoops of vanilla ice cream decoratively on top of the bananas. Chop 1 oz blanched almonds and keep on one side. Melt 2 oz good chocolate in a bowl over a pan of hot water. Add 1 tablespoon golden syrup and mix well. Pour over the ice cream, sprinkle with chopped nuts and serve.

And here's something I have since discovered which I like even more, and which I make here in my house frequently:

Banana Flambé

For two people you use 3 bananas, for four people 6 bananas. Slice them lengthways down the middle, then again in half lengthways and then cut them in the middle, so you've got eight pieces out of each banana. Take between 2–3 tablespoons demerera sugar (however it takes your fancy); ½ an orange and have a bottle of brandy to hand. Melt a little butter in a frying pan, fry the bananas until they really look a bit soggy, but they're actually beautiful tasting by that time. Mix in the demerera sugar and let them cook a little longer. Squeeze over the juice of the orange, and whizz! the pan goes. You have a friendly person standing next to you with a match, you have the bottle of brandy in your hand, you pour on a generous portion over the cooking bananas, and the friendly friend sets fire to them with a match. Blow the flames out quite quickly – otherwise the alcohol is lost – but they taste marvellous.

25

3
Variety is the Spice of Life

The kindness of the Italian family, the Pellegras, takes me back to my very first pantomime, 'Aladdin', where I met a man called Reginald Vincent. Initially he wasn't very kind to me, because he told me that the youngest person in the company had to supply sandwiches for the entire company. I believed him and spent every day looking for sandwiches, which was a bit of a problem on £3 a week! However from that poor beginning grew a lifelong friendship. I was sixteen-and-a-half then (the 'half' is always important when you're very young) and remained dearest friends with Reggie until he died a couple of years ago, when he was eighty.

He had lived for years in Italy with his mother, who had a little restaurant there at Via Reggio, and much later he and I became very interested in food, to the extent that we almost competed with each other. That was many landladies and thousands of Baked Beans and fish and chips later. We used to go to Bianchi's Restaurant in Frith Street, Soho which was about the first restaurant I'd ever been to in London. I am still friendly with *Elena*, the waitress there in those days, who is now the manageress and guiding light of L'Escargot in Greek Street. I am always so delighted when I see her. Bianchi's in those days was very inexpensive and there was a wonderful waiter called Tony who used to wail on a sort of dying note down the hatch, 'Spaghetti! Minestrone!'. He obviously resented every mouthful that you ordered, because he really wanted to eat it himself. I think he burst later in Florence – the city, I mean. Lovely Tony!

Elena, the hostess with the mostest.

Reggie was to teach me so much about Italian cooking and he really was very very interesting on the subject. He taught me some simple, but, I think, marvellous recipes. One of the first he gave me was for **Gnocchi al Romano**, an awfully good plain starter.

Gnocchi al Romano

You heat ½ pint milk and sprinkle over 2 oz semolina (here's the 'Smelly Lena' of my schooldays coming into its own)! Simmer for 10 minutes, stirring all the time. This may sound very simple, but believe me, it isn't, because it gets thicker and thicker and really becomes very hard work for your right arm – the stirring is done, of course, with a wooden spoon. Take the pan off the heat. Add salt and pepper to taste, 1 oz grated cheese and 1 beaten egg. Mix all this well, then you push it with a spoon on to a cold, flat greased plate. Put it in the fridge. When this mixture's cold enough you cut it into rounds: I usually do this with a wine glass just whatever size you want dipped in water, or those little pastry cutters you make mince pies with. You put the rounds neatly on a greased dish and you sprinkle on another 1 oz of grated cheese – I'm rather liberal with it and use more than this. Pour 1 oz melted butter over it, then bake it in a hot oven at Gas Mark 7/425°F/ 220°C until it's brown – it usually takes about 20 minutes.

Another of Reggie's rather nifty small dishes is **Eggs poached in Burgundy**.

Eggs poached in Burgundy

*Take 1 large egg per person, which you poach in half a bottle of cheap – I mean any old plonk will do – red wine. Drain, keep the egg warm and save the wine for the sauce. Fry 1 large onion, sliced into tiny little pieces, in butter with the lid on the pan until the onion goes transparent, rather than brown. When the onion has gone soft ('sweated' I think is the vulgar term that some people use), stir in 1 teaspoon flour to make a roux. Add the wine gradually and heat. Stir until this sauce thickens slightly. Then put each egg on a slice of bread, fried (in butter, of course) and pour the wine sauce over the dish. This is absolutely lovely.
P.S When I say 'butter' I mean butter or margarine – I'm not being bloody grand!*

If you're not beginning with a pasta course; I mean if you're having a light beginning (like **Cold Consommé** with a little soured cream on, and a few chives chopped on the top – that's just something that popped into my head unbidden!), a very nice main course is an Italian veal dish, **Saltimbocco** that Reggie gave me. I use English veal and never Dutch because I've seen too many films from the RSPCA ever to want to use veal from another country. When those little 'bobby calves', as they call them, have had a run for their money and are ready for the table, all you have to do is soak the slices of veal in lemon juice which takes all the colour out of them. So, in fact, all the cruelty that goes into making calves' meat very pale abroad is unnecessary as the lemon breaks any bits that aren't tender down and makes the meat the colour that people think veal should be.

Saltimbocco

For this recipe you need: 1 veal escalope per person. Bash them out with a meat hammer then cut the veal into 2 inch pieces. This dish was originally done with Parma ham, but that is now so expensive that I recommend that you use very thinly cut lean smoked back bacon. The fag of this dish is the preparation, because you have to get the pieces of bacon cut to match the size of the pieces of veal, so when you've bashed the veal out you then have to set out to make the lean bacon the same size. Take each piece of veal, put some dried sage, black pepper and salt on it and fix a piece of bacon on top with a cocktail stick. Repeat this with as many pieces as you can be bothered doing or, if you count the number of people being served you estimate perhaps four or five little pieces of veal with bacon per person, and that sort of evens it out.

You fry these, on the veal side first, for about 4 minutes, in butter/margarine/whathaveyou with a little bit of oil, so it doesn't burn the pan. Then you turn them over and fry them on the other side. You then make the frying pan very hot indeed. When it's sizzling hot pour in a glass of red wine and scrape all the bits off the bottom. Let it cook for about 2 minutes – and that's it. You can serve this with any pasta, really; I prefer tagliatelli verde. This is a lovely dish, but you must only use the best English veal, as I do. It's really worth the effort.

Still on the subject of veal, here's another favourite dish, which didn't come from Reggie, and I can't remember actually who it did come from, but I'm sure it was somebody absolutely lovely. We'll call it **Alternative Veal** – not to be confused with those comedians, who seem to be all the go.

Alternative Veal (Parmigiani)

Start by putting the oven on at Gas Mark 4/350°F/180°C. Get some English veal fillets, one per person and beat them out; if you have a meat hammer it's very useful, but if you haven't, do it carefully with a rolling pin. (I say carefully, because as rolling pins are round, they sometimes make the veal go thinner in one place than in another). Salt and pepper the fillets, dip them in beaten egg and breadcrumbs, fry them in whatever you like to use for frying, always remembering to add a little oil so it doesn't make the thing that you're frying it in burn. Put the veal to one side and keep it warm. Skin and chop 1 onion and a garlic clove and fry them in a pan. Add about 2 oz chopped bacon and a large can of tomatoes. Then add a tablespoon of flour: you blend this in to make it into a sort of thick vegetable sauce. Into the casserole you put a layer of veal fillets coated in egg and breadcrumbs, then a layer of the vegetable mixture, and a layer of grated cheese, another layer of veal, then vegetables, then cheese and so on, as far as you can, or as much as you want up the casserole . . . sounds rather funny – 'Up the Casserole!' Cook this for about 30 minutes and that should be it. On the top you put grated cheese, as much as you like, and pop it under the grill, or else just leave it in the oven for a bit longer and the cheese will bubble and go brown on the top.

Another thing I must tag on to my long association and friendship with Reggie Vincent is that he taught me how to make **Glüwein**, the lovely mulled wine that you have when you get to the top of a mountain. I made up a recipe here for four people – and you don't *have* to go to the top of a mountain before you drink it. It's more as the mood takes you.

Glüwein

For mulled wine for four people you need: 4 glasses of wine; 1 glass of water; $\frac{1}{4}$ teaspoon grated nutmeg; 8 cloves; $\frac{1}{2}$ a cinnamon stick (or, rather a cinnamon stick measuring $\frac{1}{2}$ inch); $1\frac{1}{2}$ tablespoons brown sugar; 3 slices of orange and 3 slices of lemon. Put all this into a saucepan; simmer, but don't *boil it. You heat and stir for 30 minutes to get the full flavour and you serve in those lovely pottery mugs, or whatever you have. This is absolutely ideal for those days when you're freezing cold in the winter, because you find the blood coursing through your veins – if you're not careful, out of the window. Again, you can use cheap red wine, but a full bodied one – and, oh, you'll enjoy that!*

While we're talking about drinks, I have quite a strong feeling about drinks and the sort of way you ought to deal with guests. If I ever have a small lunch party or gathering of some sort here, I make sure that the first drink is the strongest one possible, and that really starts them talking. After that, you can make them about a third as strong and nobody ever notices, which is wonderful – it really gets the whole thing going, I think. One drink I make that people do seem to like is a drink called **Negroni**:

Negroni

This has equal measures of gin, Italian sweet vermouth, dry vermouth and orange juice, and it's topped up with slices of orange, ice and soda. This really is a marvellous drink: it's quite potent, so it's pretty good starter. Another good starter is Vodka and Cinzano with soda: it doesn't seem to be strong, but it really takes its toll. When the guests settle down to eat, I normally serve dry white wine as most people I know like it – very few people now drink red wine I find. I used to love red wine; I can't drink it at all now. So it's dry white for me, then I either have Perrier water in another glass or some soda to put into the white wine.

PIMM'S AT THE APERITIF

A good few years ago – in fact in 1946, after my nine years of pantomime for Tom Arnold – I had the great pleasure of working in Scotland, in the 'Half Past Eight Shows'. First I did a season in Edinburgh and then one in Glasgow. These were seasons of about twenty-four weeks, so we worked extremely hard, and, naturally, if you work terribly hard and you're very young, you also play hard. We were crazy about having parties at one or another's digs after the show and going home at two in the morning and rattling all the dustbin lids and that sort of thing – it was perfectly harmless sort of fun to us, though perhaps the neighbours didn't always share that view.

My mother, who was Edinburgh-born, came to have a little holiday with me. I had digs in Tarvitt Street – very grand, I thought, but it wasn't grand at all; it was at the back of everywhere, behind the theatre. I had a lovely person who looked after me there – so when we got paid, which was every Friday at lunchtime, we used to go to a very swish cocktail bar called the Aperitif, in the middle of Edinburgh. I once saw John Gielgud and Mary Morris there – not together, I hasten to add – but that will give you an idea of the kind of clientele it used to boast.

One pay day I said, 'Oh, come on, Mummy; we'll go to the Aperitif

– even the name has a smart ring to it. 'Have a Pimm's – they're lovely', I suggested. They cost half a crown then and had everything in them that you could possibly imagine – I mean not like now, when they advertise Pimm's with a slice of lemon in it. Well, I'd see it in hell unless it had cucumber, mint and a cherry in it, and orange, apple and a bit of lemon. These were gorgeous-looking things and we were sitting on stools at the bar, and my mother, who had never had one before, said, 'Oh, this is rather nice, isn't it Beryl – like lemonade?' 'Oh, yes, Mummy,' I replied, knowing full well that I could only drink *one*, if I was going to get on the tram and go home.

My mother was half way through her Pimm's when a gentleman in a kilt sitting behind us who was ordering his drinks handed some money to the lady behind the bar and accidently dropped a shilling into my mother's drink. He flushed and said, 'Oh, I'm awfully sorry,' – they were all frightfully grand there – 'I'm awfully sorry, that's terrible. Oh what a shame – I'm so sorry. I must buy you another drink, of course . . .', He was hoping he'd get his shilling out, you see. My mother said, 'No, no, no, you're far too decent. No, no, it's quite all right,' and all this performance went on until she was prevailed upon to let him buy her another Pimm's. Again, he was 'Far too decent' for doing it, and she sat drinking this second Pimm's until it was time to leave. She got up to go, turned to get off the stool and fell straight onto the floor.

I sort of had to cover up for her. Of course, she didn't drink at all, and she thought that as it tasted like lemonade it must be like lemonade. So that was a slight fall from grace for my mother at the Aperitif, but it was a beautiful place and it was wonderful for us to have a little fling there on a Friday.

Pimm's of course, used to have four bases to it: Number One had the gin base, Number Two, I think was rum, Number Three was brandy and Number Four was whisky. If you ever asked for any of the other numbers in a bar today you would be, if not actually asked to leave for subversion, greeted by a look of absolute emptiness from everybody, because nobody who serves in a bar now would ever know that there were four lots of Pimm's. But I thought it was wonderful to have the choice.

'ARE YOU STILL WOKKING?'

In my very early days – in fact, when I first went into pantomime – there was an act from the Orient called the Massa Hirakawa. It was a hair-raising act with the head man swooping down from the Circle on a rope, with

Mooncat's dad, David Claridge and me after 82 programmes.

divisions in the toes of his sock so that he could stand on the rope. He was always not only blindfolded but usually blind drunk as well. I never quite worked out how he managed it without coming to grief. They were a wonderful act and lovely people and, of course they had trailers which I got invited to. Although I had yet to learn the excitement about food and cooking, I could not help but be aware that their so-different food was beautiful. The thing about Japanese or Chinese food is that the preparation does take a great deal of time. I recalled it all so well when I started cooking that way with a wok.

I gave a wok to my friend Maria Price, who is a wonderful cook. She was the designer on the television show I did for children with *Mooncat*, 'Get Up and Go', and I went to visit her in Brighton not very long ago. 'Are you still wokking?' I asked her. My accent at that moment must have taken on a Scottish tinge, because she said, 'Oh yes, we wok nearly everywhere – we hardly ever take the car!' However I know she does use her wok a lot, because these very quickly stir-fried things can be awfully tasty. With a grateful nod in the direction of the Massa Kirakawas, here is my recipe for **Chop Suey**, which translated means mixture:

Chop Suey

You need: the cooked breast of a chicken or any leftover chicken. (You see, when these meals were cooked in the country where they came from, they were peasant dishes, so everything that was left over was put in, but now we've made them much more refined and put the best sort of ingredients in, and in a way I suppose I do prefer it.); a few spring onions; 1 celery stick; 2 bamboo shoots (you can buy these canned, of course); 2 Jerusalem artichokes; 1 head of Chinese leaves; 2 oz mushrooms; 2 oz bean sprouts; 1 oz cornflour; 2 oz butter; 3 tablespoons oil; 1 pint chicken stock; 1 dessertspoon soy sauce (actually, I never measure it, I just plonk it on).

You slice all the vegetables up – this is the part that takes an awfully long time, because they must be cut up very, very finely, with no bits that are going to get in the way, like the string on the celery or anything like that. Everything is cut into thin strips, except, of course, the bean sprouts, which just stay as they are, or rather, are put in as they are. Slice the chicken meat as well. Mix the cornflour and butter well together. Heat the oil and then add all the vegetables and fry quickly for 3 minutes, stirring all the time. You then add the stock and let it cook for 3 minutes. Then add the cornflour mixture. Stir this well, add the chicken meat and soy sauce and cook for 3 minutes. Serve hot. The secret of this dish is to be able to savour the separate taste of each vegetable and they must be finely chopped and cooked very quickly. It's wonderful – that is, if you can be bothered.

Another delicious Chinese recipe I can date back to that time was:

Bean and Meat Rolls

You need 8 oz pork or veal, minced; 2 oz butter; a can of bean sprouts or, fresh if you can get them and a lot of greengrocers do have them; 1 garlic clove – skinned, chopped or put in a garlic crusher; 1 dessertspoon soy sauce; 2 oz plain flour; $\frac{3}{4}$ pint water; salt and pepper; oil for deep frying.

Melt the butter. Add the meat, bean sprouts and garlic and fry them together for 5 minutes. Then stir in the soy sauce. Put this mixture to one side to cool. Now mix the flour and the water to a smooth batter and season with salt and pepper. You heat a 6 inch frying pan, rub with butter, pour in a tablespoon of the batter that you've just made, let it spread over the pan by shaking

33

the frying pan from side to side, cook quickly for a few seconds, in fact, until it's just set and then you lift it out on to a board. You repeat this until all the batter is used up: out of this you get about twelve pancakes. As you make them put a little square of greaseproof paper between each one to keep them separate. Put about a dessertspoon of meat into all these pancakes, fold them up into little parcels. Damp the edges to seal them tightly. Drop the parcels into hot deep fat as if you were doing chips and fry them until golden brown and crisp.

SEMPRINI AND CONSUELA

At one time in my variety life I had a really splendid run with Semprini, the great pianist, whose slogan was 'Old ones, new ones'. He drove a Bedford van and his piano was in the back on foam rubber, so that it wouldn't be damaged in any way. He used to practise for six hours every day. He had a caravan at the back – or 'caraban' as his Spanish wife Consuela used to call it – and they were the most lovely people to be with. They used to invite me often to the caravan, despite the fact that he practised so long and so hard, and I learnt so much about practically everything from them, especially from the cooking point of view, as they were both experts in the kitchen, or in this case, the 'caraban'. Semprini, although born in Dudley, had been brought up in Italy, so, of course, he had several riveting Italian recipes, Consuela, as I've said was Spanish and that was her speciality. They were quite happy to take it in turns. That was, of course, a very good learning place for me. He used to do very simple things with veal – I keep saying it – the English type of veal, which I have since come to think of as:

Semprini's Veal Special

It would be cut into small fillets and beaten out, then he would season it with salt and pepper and fry very gently in butter with chopped capers. Then he would turn the pan up to be very hot before pouring in a little white wine, which made its own sauce. It had a very delicate flavour, and it was usually served with pasta and always with a glass of wine.

He also taught me how to cook:

Osso Bucco

For this you need: a knuckle of veal, cut into 2 inch pieces (you have to get the butcher to saw this up for you, because it's the *leg bone, surrounded by a circle of meat, with the bone, of course, filled with marrow); 1 garlic clove, skinned and crushed; $\frac{1}{2}$ pint stock (a chicken cube would do); 1 oz butter; a couple of tablespoons of (olive) oil; 2 oz flour; 4 tomatoes or a small can of tomatoes; half a glass of dry white wine (you see, it's always there!); chopped parsley and the rind of 1 lemon. If you're going on a bit you can have a couple of leeks in it, a Spanish onion, skinned and chopped, a head of celery, and what is rather nice is about $\frac{1}{4}$ lb lean bacon, chopped up, a little bit of thyme and half a bay leaf.*

You fry the onion, garlic and bacon and then put in the chopped leeks and celery. Season with salt and pepper, stew very slowly for about 40 minutes with the stock in a saucepan with the lid on. Then you melt the butter in a frying pan with the oil, dip the pieces of veal in the flour before putting them in the pan to brown on each side. Put the vegetables into a casserole, add the tomatoes, quartered, the wine and the rest of the stock left over from stewing the vegetables, and, lastly of course, the veal. You cook it for about $1\frac{1}{2}$ hours with the lid on in a modernate oven at Gas Mark 4/375°F/180°C. Before you serve it with rice, garnish with some chopped parsley and grated lemon rind – that helps to make it perfect, assuming all has gone swimmingly before.

Semprini and his beautiful wife Conseula were a marvellous couple and very much in love. He would buy her a beautiful fur coat and the next day she wanted something else, so he'd say to her, 'Now Consuela, it can't be Christmas every day', which, of course is quite true for all of us – it can't be.

She did teach me a great deal about Spanish cooking; again, **Paëlla** was originally a Spanish peasant dish, made up from scraps, and we've made it more refined. Here's one way to do it:

Paëlla

*First you skin and chop an onion and a garlic clove and fry them in a deep frying pan – I have on my shelf a favourite **Paëlla** pan with handles on either side, which makes it easy to swing round while you're cooking. Add 2 cupfuls of long grain rice with enough water to cover and cook gently until it is absorbed by the rice. Season with salt and pepper. Add a lovely big can of those peeled fat tomatoes which are inexpensive and save a lot of fiddling.*

35

I only like **Paëlla** with fish and use mussels, prawns and any shellfish that is available at the moment. You can of course add pork and chicken, but then it gets to be a kind of a mess of a taste to me. If you use fresh mussels you should cook them first and put them in and when you feel that they and the prawns (and if you're rich enough to add lobster or crab) are sufficiently heated through then you add, ideally, a pinch of saffron to make it a really rich orange – gold colour, because colour is very important in food. In Spain they sell a kind of imitation, which to me seems merely colouring, with very little taste. Real saffron is made from the stamen of crocuses, which is why it is so very expensive to buy, because, as you can imagine, it's a long dreary process drying the stamens of crocuses out. In fact, in a part of Spain they do have a seasonal crocus cull for just this purpose, which must be rather like 'Tulips from Amsterdam' – only they haven't put music to it – yet. A satisfactory substitute we have here is turmeric – the powdered root of an Asian plant which isn't expensive, but has quite a distinctive flavour (and can be used for medicinal purposes so it must be all right) and is near enough the right colour yellow. Add some *chopped parsley – the Spaniards often put in peas and French beans or whatever colourful vegetables they have left over.*

If you can find the right kind of pan **Paëlla** *is really quite fun to do. It looks good – and by golly, it tastes good!*

Consuela, of course, did have a lot of trouble with her English: she said, 'I am fed up of goin' into the greengrocer's shop. I ask for a pound of piss and everybody is laughin' at me!' Another problem nearer home was when the laundryman came to the door, 'I say, "There are the shits," which makes *him* laugh!' She used to get terribly het up because she couldn't quite get the pronounciation right, but I must say it was wonderful for me and I've dined out on her quite often! She gave me a lovely recipe:

Consuela's Tripe   *Cooked, of course, the Spanish way and starting as usual with skinning and chopping onions, and a garlic clove. Fry them together, then a lot of tomatoes (a can would do nicely again), also if you care for it, add a chopped green pepper. You cook that in one pan. Cut the tripe into 1 inch pieces, whatever tripe you like, be it thick seam or honeycomb or whatever you can get. You start that off by frying it in butter, margerine or oil and when it has started to give way, you transfer it to the mixture in the other pan and let it simmer, topping it up with water from time to time, or a little white wine watered down. Sometimes a teaspoon of vinegar is rather nice in it. Simmer away until the tripe is cooked. I'm sure you'll enjoy it.*

Talking of tripe reminds me of the time when I was doing Mooncat which Rick Vanes wrote the dialogues for. I kept on about how their tripe was much better than ours. When I was leaving to fly home one Friday night a gift-wrapped parcel was left for me at reception and an envelope. I opened the envelope and read the contents on the way to the airport. I can't remember the whole of the poem but the last three lines were:

> In Oldham we're poorer
> We scorn Interflora
> We put all our love into tripe

Of course when I got to the airport I had this parcel in my basket and the girl examining it said, 'What's this Beryl?' I said, 'Well, it's tripe!'

37

She said, 'I'll have to look at it.' I replied, 'Well you look out because I can't wrap it up again.' To which she answered, 'Get off!' So I took my parcel with me unopened. I thoroughly enjoyed it when I got home.

I also love tripe cooked the traditional way, and if I'm a bit nervous and having difficulty in eating what I call ordinary food then I always try to get some tripe – thick seam for preference – so here goes with:

Tripe in the Old Fashioned (English) Way

Cut 1½ lbs tripe up into small pieces. Skin and chop a couple of Spanish onions into tiny pieces. Put the tripe and onions into a pan with some water and a good deal of white pepper and, of course, salt. Let it simmer for as long as it cares to until the tripe is really very well cooked (1½ to 2 hours would not be too long). I then make a white sauce, starting with a knob of butter in the bottom of a saucepan, adding the same amount of white flour and stirring until that has got into a roux and is looking like the beginning of a white sauce. Add enough milk to make it a quite thick white sauce.

Take that off the heat and gradually add some of the liquid that the tripe has been cooked in and put it back on to the heat and stir until it's boiling. I then fish out the actual pieces of tripe and the onions and transfer them to the white sauce. Put a little more pepper in – it does need a lot of pepper – and have great joy in eating it. It's wonderful – and not very expensive and something light when my stomach is unable to take richer food.

EDDIE AND NANCY

My days with the Semprinis were during the mid-Fifties, by which time I was deeply into and riveted by cooking. But long before that I was in variety with a very strange couple called Eddie Gordon and Nancy. She had a fetish for collecting newspapers and used to go round the bomb sites collecting them late at night and put them under their bed in the digs, because Eddie had thrown them away. They were at loggerheads and she always managed to be late for everything. She used to make him sandwiches of peanut butter and jelly, and if he wouldn't eat them she used to go round the dressing-rooms trying to sell them. She was an incredible character and I don't know how they ever managed to live together. They were so different: he dressed like a tramp and was a fanatic about time and she was determined to be late. There was this terrible conflict, because she would always delay her entrance – they were the speciality before the finale of the pantomime. He was a trick-cyclist and clown and he used to get desperate because she wasn't there and he would shout 'C'm on, Nancy – the sods are singing!' These were the delightful children from the audience. He was a really desperate man. She was very elegant, but had an extraordinary brain. She came into my dressing-room one night an collapsed into a chair. I said, 'Oh, Nancy, what's the matter?' and she said, 'Aw I'm *exhausted*, I've just made a jelly!' They were one of the most fascinating couples I have ever worked with.

A CRATE OF LUNG TONIC

Another rather marvellous person I worked with, though any connection with food is purely medicinal, was Herschel 'Jizz' Henlere, who was a brilliant pianist from Belgium who always made up as a clown. He was terribly hard to get off the stage and he did things which fascinated me, like having a hankey with a rubber ball inside it on a piece of elastic on his finger and then blowing his nose and bouncing his handkerchief – those were all things I'd never seen in my life before. He used to have his accordion very craftily hidden under the piano and he would snatch that as the curtains closed and take it in front of the curtains and play the accordion, so they'd absolutely no way of getting him off. I used to suggest they threw him the keys and ask him to lock up when he'd finished!

His life pattern was quite strange: instead of ordering a crate of Guinness, which was quite likely in those days, he used to order a crate of Owbridge's lung tonic, which he seemed to enjoy thoroughly, because that was his tipple. Of course, it is full of laudanum, so I suppose it kept him very happy and spurred him on to want to go on performing to delight the populace.

BRON'S CHICKEN

In a much later pantomime (by which time Monica and Marlene were on the scene) I had a wonderful friend – at least she became my

'If you've got it, why not let 'em have it.' Me as Marlene.

friend, although unfortunately I don't hear from her at the moment. She was called Bron (I don't know if it was short for something) and she was a marvellous woman who dressed me and looked after me on frequent visits to Coventry. I did two pantomimes there, but I also did a Spring Show with Jimmy Edwards. The first panto was 'Aladdin' (who was Eve Boswell – her recipe was 'Pickin' a Chicken' and I didn't quite dig that) but Bron was wonderful, because I used to do this long drive home every Saturday night on the M1 and plus (you have to go on the M45 to get to it). I did it for so many years that I go all numb when I think about it. Bron used always to cook me a chicken which she gave me to take home so I didn't have to cook on Sunday because I got very tired, as we did two performances every day for the first eight weeks. These are tiny little runs that they do now, and they wonder what's hit them, but it was very hard and tough in those days – sometimes even into the end of April or beginning of May. You spent your whole day there – no time to go back to the digs – and sweet kind and lovely Bron used to produce this bird, which was always on a plate, so it used to be called 'Bron's chicken on Bron's plate' and people wondered what I was taking home – a Bronze chicken on a Bronze plate! I was eternally grateful to her because it did save me so much trouble when I got home.

Bron lived in Coventry and I think she was born there. I did another panto when she looked after me, with Ken Dodd. As I have remarked before, I called it 'Waiting for Doddo', because I wasn't really let on a lot. He was another one who had to be thrown the keys and told to lock up. I think some people want medals for staying on longest, but I must say he was an extremely funny man and the audience adored him. I sometimes had other views, because I spent too long waiting in the wings, or in the dressing-room. But Bron and the lady door-keeper Nan really looked after me (dear Nan has since died) and the other compensation was that this was the first time I'd had a long stay in a posh hotel. The Leofric had opened in Coventry and I thought how absolutely marvellous it was to be staying in such a lovely hotel, and it was really living in luxury.

My mother came to stay and it was the time when the pantomime ball was going to be on and she said, 'Of course, Beryl, I won't be staying long at the ball'. She had just got settled in at the ball and the lady Mayor, Pearl Hyde, gave her a bouquet and my mother really got quite carried away, and was dancing the night away much more than I ever possibly could. I'd ordered her supper in her bedroom, and I'd got her half a bottle of champagne and some cold lobster. In fact, she didn't really go up to her bedroom until four o'clock in the morning. There I found her, sitting up in bed, drinking the champagne and eating the lobster and saying, 'You know, Beryl, I think I could take to this life'.

FAT FISH

I did work, too, with some absolutely brilliant and very elegant oriental people doing plate spinning on those thin cane rods. I could never make out however they did all these beautiful things with whizzing coloured ribbons, making patterns on the stage: they were always very artistic. I rather think they were Japanese, and in their trailer I saw a wonderful way that they cooked fish. They had to be fairly small fish – what they called 'round fish' I understand what they mean by that – a plaice is flat, lemon sole is flat, but these were like red mullet would be – fish with a rounded middle, but short in length. I couldn't tell you exactly what sort of fish they used, but I see them frequently in fishmongers – lots of little fishes with fat tummies. Of course, you have to clean them out first.

I've got a very old-fashioned steamer, so I'm lucky (I don't mean a steamer you take on the ocean, of course, but a steamer for the cooker) which was given to me by my old friend Reggie Vincent, and it fits on three different sizes of saucepan, but it is an old-fashioned gadget. You can now buy them made of sort of wickerwork, with a wooden frame and a lid, at oriental shops in Chinatown, Gerrard Street, or at oriental supermarkets. There seem to be so many of them about now.

This is the way my plate-spinning friends cooked this lovely fish dish.

Oriental Fat Fish   *Have some water boiling in a saucepan and place the steamer over it. Line the bottom of the steamer with spring onions, lay the fish on the bed of spring onions and on the top you place thin slices of fresh root ginger. In between each slice you put a slice of lemon or lime – a citrus fruit, not orange, because that would take the beautiful flavour away from it. You steam the fish until it's cooked – a gentle testing with a fork will tell you this if you're not certain from the look of it. You then lift the fish off the bed of spring onions and pour very hot fat over it which really crisps it up. Place the pieces of ginger back on top with some new slices of lemon or lime. Grate a little nutmeg over the top of it, then dress it up with the green shoots of the spring onions and sprinkle each one with soy sauce, to look really eye-catching. I must say the flavour is memorable.*

41

4
Haute Cuisine with Harry, The Horns and Dick Whittington

'We've never had it so good,' said Harry Secombe to me at the London Palladium in 1956. He was not referring to the show, although it was a smashing one, with Winifred Atwell and Alma Cogan both also in the company – in fact it was the caviar we were spooning into our mouths in the dressing-room from shoe-horns I'd been able to dredge up from my make-up case. Harry had his hair parted in the middle as the simpleton son of a hideous crone with lank locks, and that was yours truly, when I thought I really had made it to the Mecca of all variety theatres, in the West End.

THE HORNS

It was during this show that I became friendly with the mother of Rudy Horn, Val Parnell's new young discovery, a teenage and very clever unicyclist with flame-coloured hair and a sense of balance that quite took your breath away. The Horns were German and Rudy's mother and I got on awfully well because she was a fine cook and we were able to swap recipes. We did have trouble though with some of the ingredients because it was very hard to translate the things that she could buy into the things that I understood. We did really very well, all the same – she taught me how to make **Borscht**, that beautiful dish that's actually Russian, although they do make it in Germany.

Personalities in "ROCKING THE TOWN"

HARRY SECOMBE
WINIFRED ATWELL
ALMA COGAN
HOLGER & DOLORES
BERYL REID
GENE DETROY and MARQUIS FAMILY
TRIO FREDIANI

One of the happiest shows.

Borscht

For two people you would need 1 lb shin of beef; whole uncooked beetroot; a carrot and an onion, skinned and sliced; salt and pepper (of course I like black pepper in those sort of things). Cover the ingredients with water and simmer until the meat and the beetroot are properly cooked and you feel that you have really got all the good out of the meat. For the actual soup you remove the meat, the carrot and the onion, but you skin the beetroot when it's cooked and cold. Grate the beetroot into the soup, which makes it a wonderful colour. The soup is lovely served with a little dollop of soured cream on the top. (If you can't actually get soured cream – and I think most stores stock it these days – you just use ordinary cream of any kind, even top of the milk, and squeeze a bit of lemon into it and it automatically becomes soured cream). Then grind some black pepper on top of that.

This is a beautiful soup, which you can have either hot or cold. Start with this then, if you keep the meat warm, you can cut it into slices, which are full of glutinous goodness and make a caper sauce. This is white sauce, with a little vinegar and chopped capers added. Pour this over the meat. Boiled potatoes are very nice with this, so you've got the beauty of the soup, done with the vegetables, then a lovely main dish as well. It really is something to write home about – and so simple to prepare.

Another thing Mrs. Horn taught me, which was very economic and terribly tasty was how to make her **Potato Pancakes**.

Potato Pancakes

This is best when old potatoes are available. Peel and grate, on a coarse grater, because it goes an awful long way, a couple of big old potatoes or three medium-sized ones. Then leave them in the fridge covered up for a little while. Squeeze the mixture with a spoon and pour away the liquid – quite a lot comes out of them. They lose their colour a bit, but don't let this upset you, because it doesn't show in the finished product. You then add, depending on the amount of potatoes either a dessertspoon or a tablespoon of plain flour, a garlic clove, peeled and crushed and an egg and you mix all this up together. Heat some fat in the frying pan – I actually only use a teaspoon, because it goes such a long way. Get the fat really quite hot and put a large teaspoonful or a large dessertspoonful of the mixture into the frying pan, then press this little pancake thing with the back of the spoon so that all the little bits of potato flute out at the sides and make a very pretty sort of shape, all spikey round the edges. You can get about twenty of these little things out of two potatoes and they taste wonderful; also it's an unusual way of cooking potatoes and a way that people are not usually au fait *with. The Jewish people cook these potatoes, too, but without the garlic. You have to be sure to press them practically flat with the back of the spoon as you put the mixture into the frying pan, and they have to be cooked until they're brown and crisp and flutey. It takes between 7–10 minutes to do: certainly no longer and probably much less, but I never properly count time or really measure things.*

Rudy's mother was a real expert on the simple and economical ways of cooking that were tasty and unusual. One of her recipes that follows is terribly easy to do.

Potato Salad with Rollmops

You need: 2 medium potatoes; 2 tablespoons olive oil; 1 table-spoon wine vinegar; gherkins; salt and pepper; parsley; 4 roll-mops. Boil the potatoes in their skins – when you do this they have a special waxy sort of feel, then peel and slice them before you use them. While they're still warm, dress them with the oil and the vinegar. Slice the gherkins and add them to this salad. Season with salt and pepper, sprinkle with chopped parsley and sit the rollmops on the top, so you can have a serving of rollmop with the potato salad underneath it. That looks pretty, too.

My German friend also gave me a superlative recipe for **Sauerkraut**.

Sauerkraut

You can't buy it from the barrels here like you can on the continent, where you just say, I'd like half a pound of that, please – or whatever you require. Here you can get it in cans. You start off by frying – it seems as though I've never got the frying pan out of my hand, but that isn't true at all! – a chopped onion and a peeled crush garlic clove. Then when the onion and garlic are cooked, add the sauerkraut, then just turn it over for a little while without adding any liquid, so that you mix the onion and the garlic and the sauerkraut all together. When it begins to look as if it's cooking, add ½ pint beer of any sort – be it lager or brown beer. Season with salt and pepper. Then get the mixture to simmering point of the beer and put in a dessertspoonful or two of demerera sugar according to taste (I say that because the quality of brown sugar varies so much these days; I think some of it is just dyed white sugar) and a couple of bay leaves. Let it cook for about ¾ hour and keep turning it every 15 minutes (you have to watch the level of the liquid) until it has practically all cooked away yet is just moist enough and hot enough. Have it with a couple of Frankfurter sausages or a boiled ham hock, and it's so lovely you'd just be anybody's!

LOBSTER ON THE FIRE ESCAPE

Harry Secombe, since that Palladium show, has become a lifelong friend of mine and he did ask me to be on his Sunday programme, 'Highway'. It was a terrible day: I went to Reading and it was thick with snow, and that was before I'd got my moon boots. So, of course, I was tottering about in silly girls' shoes, looking like a big girls' blouse, having lunch with him on board some ship. Another boat came alongside and I wondered what it was: of course, it was the one with the food on, which kept delivering the lunch to us, which was really quite funny.

It was lovely to see Harry again; he's always been Mr. Wonderful Guy, and a year at the Palladium with him was quite an exceptional part of my life. I used to buy lobsters on the way in on a Saturday (we did twice-nightly and three shows on Saturday) and I'd have a bottle of Chablis at home which I kept as cold as possible in the fridge, because I hadn't got a fridge in the dressing-room, so I used to put the lobster out on the fire escape and the Chablis wherever I thought it would keep coldest, even if it was soaking in cold water, and that was our 'high tea' between the first show and before the two evening shows.

It wasn't long after that he introduced me to friends who came round to see him as Val Parnell's mother!

It really was the essence of our relationship that phrase, 'We never had it so good'. I was trying to remember how much the lobsters cost – very little indeed and I used to get them in a fish shop on the way to the theatre which is no longer in existence. Now, if I go to my fishmonger in Chiswick, Mr. Portch, a middling-sized lobster, that would do for one very hungry person or two not so hungry people, with a lot of things with it, like potato salad and a green salad and all those other nice things and mayonnaise would be about £5.50. I was goggle-eyed the other day, looking at the television – not from over-indulgence in the box, more from shock, really –

on one of the programmes where the Farmhouse Kitchen had gone to a fishmonger who was so knowledgable and so deft it was absolutely wonderful and there was a lobster there that was about £19.50. There the imagination boggles and you just have to stop thinking about lobsters, unless you take a mortgage out.

But to get back to Harry Secombe, I did do 'This Is Your Life', which I've no doubt some of you have seen over the years, because so many people's lives have been done. It was rather nice for me to be on this programme, particularly, because my brother Roy died and the recording for the programme is the only recorded sound of his voice we've got. I've given the actual book with all the photographs to his wife Pat, who lives in the Wirral peninsula. I didn't know who was going to appear on the programme – you think nobody is, because you suddenly get so depressed on that drive to London, thinking everybody you know is dead! They had all sorts of surprises for me and they showed Harry on film – you know, those little clips that come on – he had sent me a jereboam of champagne and, of course they had it in the studio. I was sitting open mouthed at the look of this bottle and suddenly it was wheeled onto the stage. I thought, 'Oh, lovely – toff's lemonade!' then nearly passed out at the size: it was almost as big as me. But it was a wonderful thought and it was absolutely lovely of him to do it for me (I practically had to be wheeled out at the look of it) and just another one of those beautiful things that we've enjoyed together.

TOMMY COOPER AND THE ITCHING POWDER

Humour of a very different kind was rife in the last pantomime I've done to date – I'd say positively the last, except that life and show business are full of surprises – and that was 'Dick Whittington' at Golders Green, with Gary Miller in the title role, a very handsome, lovely man who died of a heart attack tragically young and Tommy Cooper who, sadly went the same way last year. You see the names on a poster and you have to remind yourself that they're not still with us and that you can't have a laugh or lift a glass together.

Laughter, of course, was Tommy's forte, almost his reason for living, and he had quite an extraordinary sense of humour. He brought itching powder to rehearsals and then when we'd kind of taken that in our stride, twitching a little, he brought sneezing powder from his joke shop, which was, of course, not very much appreciated by all the cast, as you can imagine, although it cleared our heads for a while. Then he would insist on coming into my dressing-room – we were very friendly, but he would insist on doing conjuring tricks for me. I said, 'I don't like conjuring tricks; please don't do them here'! He said, 'Oh, you're just like Dove, my wife – she doesn't like conjuring tricks – she won't let me do them anywhere'! Poor Tommy – but, like my mother said, when the new-fangled moving staircase deposited her and her four sisters, my aunts Belle, Liza, Agnes and Jenny on the floor of a big store in Ayr because they had no idea how to get off, 'We all had a thoroughly good laugh about it afterwards'!

Tommy told me that his wife made cheesecake 'Oh, how wonderful,' I said, 'Do you think she'd give me the recipe?' Now, I had tried for years, to make a really good cheesecake. I'd experimented with all sorts of recipes – I'd done it with raisins on pastry (that was the Polish way) I'd tried every sort of way, but it was never, in my opinion, any kind of a success at all. I said to Tommy Cooper, 'Oh, I do *wish* I could make good cheesecake.' So here's Dove's recipe which was a great success.

Dove's Cheesecake

I must say you can't fail with this. You need: 1 packet of Lyons sponge cakes; 1 lb curd cheese; 4 tablespoons caster sugar (actually I only use two); 2 eggs; $\frac{1}{2}$ pint double cream; a knob of butter; 1 teaspoon cornflour and I add a little lemon juice to this (I don't know what I'd do without lemon juice, but lemons are so expensive it's ridiculous and you almost grudge putting them into things, although everything benefits from them).

First of all you get an 8 inch cake tin, you know the kind with a loose bottom that you can push up when it's cooked, and it looks rather lovely: you line this tin with the sponge cakes, cut into as thin slices as possible, but the sugary bits you put to one side, because you decorate it with those afterwards. You line the tin and then you mix the curd cheese, sugar, the eggs, cream, butter, cornflour, and the lemon juice together, and pour into the tin. You have to be careful to keep the bits of sponge cake at the side of the tin. I sort of swear and have to take them out and put them back again if they slide into the middle. You just have to have a lot of hands at the time ready to keep them to the side. Crumble the little bits of sugary stuff off the top of the sponge cake – just sort of scrunch them up in your hands – and scatter then over the top of the cheesecake – to – be and, funnily enough, they do look beautiful. You bake this mixture at Gas Mark 4/ 350°F/180°C for 1 hour and then you leave the oven to cool.

47

ANGIE

In this same pantomime there was a lovely girl called Angie who was studying at the Central School of Acting, and, of course, these were the Christmas holidays and she was dressing me as a little job while she was on vacation. She was Jewish and, I think, went to Israel to join the fighters shortly after.

I've caught up with her since: I got terribly fond of her – she really is a great big-hearted lovely girl and now, I think, has a little girl of her own. We've never crossed paths again, although I have had several letters from her. She had several relatives – a mother and aunts who made wonderful Jewish food, and she gave me two recipes for **Gefillte Fish**.

Gefillte Fish

The trick is to get mixed pieces of fish: a bit of bream, a bit of cod, a bit of herring, maybe a bit of haddock – whatever is not expensive, and if you can get it skinned and filleted, so much the better. We're talking about a large amount of mixed fish – 3 pounds, but, of course you can do it with much less, depending on how many little cakes of **Gefillte Fish** *you want. Ask the fishmonger to keep the heads, skins and bones for you. 'Take 3 eggs', as Mrs. Beaton would have said, only in her case it would more likely have been at least a Baker's Dozen and I always have a vision of a gloved hand reaching out stealthily to snatch them away from under the poor hen – take 3 eggs, 3 little onions, 2 carrots, 1 stick of celery, some chopped parsley, ground almonds, breadcrumbs, and, of course, the old salt and pepper. Put the heads, the skins and the bones of the fish in a pan with $\frac{1}{2}$ pint water, 1 sliced carrot, onions, chopped celery and salt and pepper. Simmer this for about 45 minutes, then strain it, reserving the stock. Next, mince the fish together well, with parsley, ground almonds to taste, beaten eggs and enough breadcrumbs to keep it all stuck together. Add some of the onion that has been simmering with the fish heads which gives a very nice flavour to the little fish cakes, and roll the mixture into small balls. Simmer these gently in the fish stock with the second sliced carrot for 1 hour. Remove the balls from the stock, and arrange some sliced carrot on the top of each, reducing the stock, if necessary. Pour a little of the stock over each of the Gefillte Fish cakes and it should set when cold. Of course this dish is wonderful served cold, and it's lovely with a relish that you can buy in most delicatessens (and, of course, particularly Jewish ones), horseradish and beetroot mixed together.*

48

Angie also let me into the secret of what I think of as **Angie's Chopped Liver Pâté** which I always think I can eat, but I feel slightly sick if I do!

Angie's Chopped Liver Pâté

You need: 1 lb chicken's liver; or calves liver (or you can mix them, actually, but I like it better with chicken's liver); 1 onion; 2 hard-boiled eggs; salt and pepper; 2 oz breadcrumbs; 1 oz chicken fat. (Now, you see, most Jewish people don't have roasted chickens like we do; they have boiling fowls, which in my opinion have much more flavour than an ordinary roasting fowl, unless you add a great deal to it, so this is obviously the chicken fat off the top of the water in which they've boiled the fowl.) Fry the liver lightly in the chicken fat, skin and mince the onion finely. Add the hard-boiled eggs, chopped up very finely. Season with salt and pepper. Mix in the breadcrumbs. Beat the mixture together until smooth. Sometimes people put a little layer of the chicken fat on the top – I think that's what done me in. You should serve this cold, on very thin toast: it's beautiful, but for my taste it's very rich. Thanks, Angie – thanks a bundle!

5
Loaves and Fishes

This takes me to the time when I became very keen and obsessed with Old Time Music Hall, having been several times to the City Varieties at Leeds to do the Good Old Days and where I wore all those lovely clothes. I was amazed to find there was a two years' waiting list to be a member of the audience. You had to wait to dress up in those beautiful Victorian or Edwardian clothes and come in horse-drawn cabs to the theatre.

I quite got into the swing of it and became friendly with a lot of people at the Players. I'd known Denis Martin, who has been the guiding light there for a long time now, ever since we did the revue 'The World's the Limit' at the Theatre Royal, Windsor. I've always called him 'Dublin Dick' and have difficulty remembering that his proper name is Denis Martin. He's given me so much help, letting me rehearse at the Players with the lovely pianist, Geoffrey Brawn, submitting numbers that he thought might be good for me for Old Time Music Hall, and letting me borrow clothes, like the Tramp clothes for 'I Live in Trafalgar Square'. I'm forever borrowing those, and I'm sure I would do so again, should the occasion ever arise or anyone ask me to sing it again. He always used to get me sort of 'set up' to go to Leeds for these Old Time Music Hall shows.

HIGH TEA AT HONEYPOT

In the summer of 1964, we were going to do a show at the Theatre Royal, Windsor, which, of course, is practically on my doorstep. Henry Hall's son, Mike Hall, was actually in business at that time with Johnny Hewer, who does all those wonderful adverts for Fish Fingers, the Captain's Table and Fisherman's Pie and all those sort of things. They were in the Victorian Music Hall show in which I did 'We Live In Trafalgar Square' for the first time with a man called Johnny Heawood. He was tall and thin and lugubrious and marvellously sympathetic to work with.

I was in love with the whole cast – it was a terribly happy show and I used to go backwards and forwards from Honeypot on my *bicycle*. One day I thought I must have them all out to the house because it was such nice weather, ideal for entertaining by the river. So I set to work and made great pies, out of nothing, mind you, like pigeon pies and giblet pies and steak and kidney pies. Just like the miracle of the loaves and fishes I magicked up an enormous amount of food – it's amazing what you can do if you try – I don't know how I ever managed it, and I don't think I could do it all now. Then I made boys' trifle to follow – all men love trifle and they suddenly become boys, sloshing their great big spoons in the trifle and carrying on regardless.

I asked all the cast to come over for a sort of tea after the matinee, it was an absolutely wonderful day and I had four gallons of red wine – it really was a *very* High Tea. The actors were true to form. As I've said before, actors always behave as if every meal is the Last Supper, because

the minute your engagement is finished you become 'redundant' and think you're never going to be asked to work again. People have only lately been discovering what it is be be redundant – we're redundant every time the show comes to an end. This is why they have to eat everything in sight in case it's the very last time they're going to eat: it's a sort of terrible mental block.

Anyway, it was a lovely day and all the doors and windows were open and everyone was tucking in. There they all were on the lawn and up trees – it was a riveting sight, like one of those idyllic picnic scenes from an Edwardian play. In the company was a delightful girl called Violetta, who I think originally played the French maid in 'The Boy Friend'. She's verry français and verry 'Oh, la, la!' and married to Herbert Farjeon's son Gervaise. I must say I loved her – I thought she was 'un peu drôle', but a wonderful character. I'd got all this 'all right' food ready for the cast, who were attacking it like vultures when she came up and said, 'Have you a leetle garleec, pliss?' She went on to say that she had brought her own food – a couple of chops, which she was going to cook privately in the kitchen, and 'a leetle salade, which I have preparée'.

I think she was bitterly sorry, because everybody else was enjoying the other food and she was a little left out, sitting with two tiny little chops which she was grilling all by herself in the kitchen and a bit of lettuce and a bit of garlic, while we were in the dining room with the doors and windows open tucking into a huge great cold meal. Some of the cast were sitting up trees eating and some were noshing on the lawn, while others were sitting in the little quarter of a circle seat. Everyone was having a marvellous time – no sight of the four gallons of wine – that had all gone, rattling down their gullets. I must say I lost more knives and forks that day than I've ever done in my life, because as the cast went up the trees and sat up there eating, I'm sure odd pieces of cutlery must have plummeted down into the waters beneath. Maybe an enterprising diver might come up with quite a rewarding hoard. It was a bizarre sight, really, and the show went with a *great* swing that evening. I really had made a lot of food made out of practically nothing, and I seem to have a bit of a talent for that.

MAGICKING MEALS OUT OF THE AIR

I think I've always been able to concoct a meal out of the air if people call unexpectedly, though they don't often, because my friends know how much I hate it. However, if I've got a bit of yoghurt, a few leeks and a bit of chicken stock, then I can make Vichyssoise soup. I pop out into the garden and pick a few chives and put those and a bit of top of the milk on top of the cold soup and shove it in the fridge while we're talking. I can always cook some spaghetti or tagliatelli verde with tomatoes – a can it may have to be if I don't have any fresh ones – onion rings and so on, and I can always make a **Salade Niçoise** at the drop of a hat:

Salade Niçoise

Usually in the summer there's lettuce growing in the garden and tomatoes, and I've always got cans of anchovies, and I can do a hard boiled egg to slice with the tomatoes. Before laying the anchovies on top of the lettuce, tomatoes and egg I can always whizz up some **French dressing**, *for which I have a rather nice recipe:*

I use equal quantities of vinegar, red wine, lemon juice and oil. If you make it in a little bottle – perhaps one of those olive oil miniatures you can usually get at your corner grocers – you can see the actual layers as you pour them in because they're all different colours and they each come to their own level. You want roughly the same amount of each one, then you add a drop or two of Lea and Perrins sauce, a bit of made-up English Colman's mustard, an equal quantity of salt and sugar and a garlic glove, crushed: I'm mad on my garlic crusher, but if you don't have one you can always busk, as we say in the theatre when we mean improvise. You can do it by cutting the clove in two pieces and using the back of a knife handle to press it down and extract the juice that way, which is much more effective than just cutting it into tiny pieces. You shake the mixture up and in 4 minutes flat you have your dressing.

If you're hard pressed, you can really make something out of nothing and just reach out and find something that is edible. This is just something that has come with a lot of years of cooking, so I don't panic if somebody shows up at the door unexpectedly. As I said before, I wish they wouldn't, however glad I may be to see them – but if they do, I'm ready for them!

A SIZZLING DIET

I have been reminded recently that I was once on some sort of a diet – it was during a summer season in Margate – and it included a certain brand of very heavily advertised lemon juice. I happened to spill some on my dressing-room table, and, to my horror, when I looked down, it had burnt a hole in the table. I can't imagine what it had done to my stomach. I'm still here to tell the tale, so I suppose it was just one of those spectacular things that happen to me from time to time! This incident wouldn't have been so bad if I hadn't been telling Eric Braun, who's again here helping me with this book, how terribly good this diet was, in my most serious voice and anticipating all the marvellous results I was going to get. I really felt a bit of a fool, especially as I'd advised him to try it if necessary, and there he was, staring down at the smoking hole in the dressing-table!

PICNICS IN HOLLYWOOD

My second visit to Hollywood – the first was for 'Star' with Julie Andrews – was to play the name part in 'The Killing of Sister George'. When we first went to the Robert Aldrich studios, which had been refurbished after last being used by Mary Pickford for her Independent Film Company in 1913, we found them absolutely lovely, except for the fact that there was no canteen or commissary, as they call it. On the opening day of the film we were all given presents of picnic baskets and when we asked, 'Where do we go to eat?' we were told, 'You'll have to use the picnic baskets!' It was a rather tough way of learning, as you had to be up at five o'clock to cook the food and shove it in the picnic basket and get the salads and things done before you left to be at the studio by half past seven.

I got quite used to this and the mornings there were so beautiful it really didn't matter, so when I was going round the fabulous Farmers' Market, where you could get absolutely everything, I used to get my trolley completely loaded with food to put in the fridge when I got back. I hadn't got a freezer, so it had to be used fairly quickly. Even on the way home from the Studios, which were in down-town Hollywood, you could pop into a supermarket and get almost anything you wanted, although there wasn't quite as big a choice as at the Farmers' Market, which really was a sight for sore eyes. Funnily enough, though there was plenty of everything when I got back, it rather made England – and I couldn't live anywhere else – seem as if we'd just finished the war! We looked rather poverty-stricken in comparison.

I always thought I was just going to be taking my own lunch down to the studios, but I'm a fool, because by this time (just like one of those MI5 leaks) it had got about that I brought food with me. In the end I had Coral Browne, Susannah York, Hugh Paddick (when he joined the company) and Bill Beckley (William Beckley, who became one of my very best

*Myself, Hugh Paddick and Coral Browne at
the opening night of the film of 'The Killing
of Sister George'.*

My first birthday cakes made in the shape of 3 reels of film. With Robert Aldrich.

chums when I first went to Hollywood, and who now plays the butler in 'Dynasty') all sitting around anywhere they could find in the caravan, which I mystified Robert Aldrich by calling my Wendy House. I ended up cooking for eight or nine people – loaves and fishes again!

A great stand-by of those days was roast squab, which is a small bird, perhaps a little larger than a seagull, and quite a favourite in America, where they are plentiful. There is no point in going into recipes here, because squab is no longer known in Britain, although the old recipe books do contain ways of cooking it, so it must have been known here once upon a time. With squab it was a case of salad – all kinds of salad.

A BUN IN THE OVEN

The character I played in my next film 'Entertaining Mr. Sloane' was as different from butch Sister George as it was possible to be: Kath was a wonderfully dotty 'maturing' nymphet who was absolutely crazy about her young lodger, Mr. Sloane, and, in fact, about any young boys. I don't think she had much idea about what to do with fishes, but her own version of a loaf – to boot a bun – did come to figure very large in her life. Her vision of cooking was strictly limited, I think. When Mr. Sloane told her, 'I've just kicked the Dadda very hard – in fact, I think I've killed him,' she said, 'Oh, Mr. Sloane, you shouldn't say things like that – you're not that sort of young man. Would you like a boiled egg?' So that was about

Poor Kath with her bun in the oven.

Myself and dearest Siân.

"GIGI"

1981.

To Beryl
With so much
love from the
Tall, crippled
Sister Siale x

the extent of her cooking, and the Dadda was always seen in the kitchen, eating enormous pickled onions. When she was pregnant by Mr. Sloane she lifted her very frilly pinny up and said to her brother Ed, 'You see, Ed, I've got a bun in the oven!' So, in case this inspires you to think of making a bun, here's a recipe for one!

Rich Rock Cake Bun

You need: 8 oz plain flour; 5½ teaspoons baking powder; 5 oz margarine; 5 oz sugar; 1 egg; just enough milk to mix this lot; 6 oz dried fruit; 2 oz candied peel. Sift the flour and baking powder together – you know, rattle it through a sieve. Rub in the margarine, add the sugar and the beaten egg and enough milk to make this into a stiff consistency. You must be careful not to make the mixture too soft, or the buns will kind of spread out (a bit like Kath!), particularly in this richer recipe. Add the fruit and the peel. Grease and flour a patty tin – one of those baking tins with little dips in them in which you cook mince pies or buns – and you put a little dollop of the mixture into each greased hollow. Bake near the top of the oven in a very hot oven – Gas Mark 8/425°F/220°C – for 10 minutes, lowering the heat if necessary after 5 minutes. There's your Rock Buns for you and if you want a Bun in the Oven – that's the way to get one!

As Kath liked to please the boys so much, here is something that she would certainly have had to go out and buy, if she wanted to gladden her lodger's heart. I call it **Boys' Pudding** because boys of all ages love it. You can bet your life that something men really enjoy is a Jolly Good Trifle:

Boys' Pudding

I start off with those Lyons Sponge cakes in the bottom. Take the sugary bit off the top, because you can use that for decoration. Over the sponge I pour whatever alcohol is available – brandy's good, sherry's wonderful (I don't actually like sherry very much, but it's wonderful in the bottom of a trifle). Drain a can of apricots, and put in a good layer of the fruit, cut up fairly small. Use about half the can for this. You can really put whatever you like into trifle. Then I add a layer of some yellowish jelly of some sort – you can't get apricot-flavoured jelly as far as I know, but an orange jelly tastes equally nice, and you let that start to set in the fridge before putting it on top of the sponge which will have absorbed the alcohol. After that I add a layer of custard. You can either use home-made custard with a little more sherry added but I mainly use ordinary custard, which will set, in a layer on top of the jelly. So in your beautiful glass bowl, or whatever you like to use – I happen to have a rather lovely one that Norman Newell, my MD and friend, gave me – you have layers of sponge cake, orange jelly, the custard and the apricots all set and looking very pretty. On the day I'm going to serve the trifle I add a layer of cream. Then, if I have time – and this is the whole essence of the thing – I cut the remaining half of the can of apricots to look like sunflowers in little tiny pieces all the way round the dish and I use the sugar bits off the sponge cakes to make the seed part of the sunflower, which is the centre. I can guarantee that if I've got some chaps there, the trifle will be gone in a flash! It goes a long way, if you don't let them have too many helpings.

'LITTLE AND LARGE'

It was a real pleasure when I was preparing this book to hear from one of my very special friends, Siân Phillips. Not only did we have such fun together playing sisters in the musical 'Gigi' – we laughed most of the time and used to think of ourselves as 'Little and Large', because I'm so short and she so tall – but we became what Auntie Mame referred to in her song as 'Bosom Buddies'. Siân contributed handsomely to my last book

The Cat's Whiskers, and has taken time off from a gruelling rehearsal schedule for her new play 'Thursday's Ladies' with Dorothy Tutin (to whose daughter Amanda Waring we were aunties in 'Gigi') and another 'best friend', as we used to say at school, Eileen Atkins, to write to me with a favourite recipe. Siân writes:

> *'I love adventure stories, so imagine how pleased I was when Cyril Cusack and I were asked to read his selection of Prose and Poetry for Hammond Innes' 'With Great Pleasure' programme, broadcast, to my delight, from one of my favourite places, Norwich. It was a day of pleasure for me, not least when Mrs. Hammond Innes turned out to be a soul-mate of a gardener and the sort of cook that you and I like best; one who cooks what is naturally in season in the garden.*
>
> *I'm a good Welsh woman but I prefer eating leeks to wearing them; in fact I and my family love eating them. Here is Dorothy Hammond Innes' recipe for fresh young leeks. I make it often, with old leeks as well, because it's as easy to make as part of a buffet for thirty as it is as a supper for two. There's never a scrap left over, so over-cater a bit:*

Leeks

> *To wash the leeks: cut the roots off well. Cut the green tops off. Slash down the sides of the leeks. Turn the leeks upside-down in a jug of cold water with some salt in case there are any wigglies. All the grit from them falls to the bottom of the jug.*
>
> *Allow a large helping of leeks per person and enough sauce just to cover the vegetables. Cut the leeks into 1 inch chunks, letting the tap flow freely over them until all grit is washed away. Steam till barely tender. Drain them and put them in a flameproof (gratin-type) dish. Cover with tunny sauce – a white sauce into which you've mixed flaked, canned tuna fish. Sprinkle with breadcrumbs (optional), grated cheese and brown under the grill or in the top of an Aga.*

She tells me that, apart from rehearsing (Saturdays and Sundays as well), she's been gardening and re-doing bookshelves. She ends, 'Much too tired to do acting!' Well, I'm not surprised. Love and so many thanks, Siân.

6
Food on the Move

*O*ne of the most exciting things, and one of the easiest things to do, because it's totally carefree, is to live in a caravan, and, when I was between marriages that was what I did, we had the caravan between Windsor and Maidenhead, and Hattie Jacques, who was a great friend of mine – we worked together for four years in 'Educating Archie' – used to come to visit me there. I can't remember what I cooked for her, but she was the most wonderful cook and she also had very easy ways of doing things.

Everybody always makes such a fuss about making a soufflé, but Hattie made me understand that it was really very easy. At the time she was

Hattie and John with their sons Robin and Kim in my caravan at Margate.

Here I am, posing again.

explaining it to me I was trying to put some screws in the wall and I joked, 'I suppose John does *all* this for you, Hattie?'. She said, 'Let's face it, Darling, John doesn't do *anything!*' I so loved John LeMesurier, who was then her husband, but I had a little laugh about that. She showed me how terribly easy it was to make a **Cheese Soufflé**, or whatever kind of soufflé you fancied.

Cheese Soufflé

Simply make a white sauce, from 1 oz butter, 1 oz flour and $\frac{1}{4}$ pint of milk, and add a couple of ounces of grated cheese, therefore making it into a cheese sauce. Take the pan off the heat and when it's getting a bit cooler add the yolks of 2 eggs. Then, if you were feeling very flush, you could whisk up the whites of 3 eggs (but 2 would do) and when they were stiff, fold them into the cheese sauce. Mind you, I don't just leave it as cheese sauce; I put a little bit of Lea and Perrins sauce in it, a dash of lemon juice, salt and pepper, and, if I have the will to walk to the end of the garden I cut a few chives off and put those in – they look rather pretty in the mixture, then I put a few on the top as well.

Having folded the stiff egg whites into the mixture, you then pour it into a greased soufflé dish, this really means anything that is a little bit tall at the sides and about 8 inches across. Then pour the mixture into the dish. Cook it at Gas Mark 4/350°F/180°C for about 35 minutes or until the soufflé has risen up and gone a bit brown on the top, and got a few cracks in it. Stick a knife into it to make sure that the knife comes out clean and then its well and truly done.

It is terribly easy – the only thing that isn't easy to do is to find yourself in the kitchen when the guests are arriving because the soufflé should be eaten when it is just cooked, or it is inclined to go sort of kerflounk in the middle, which is a pity, because it looks so wonderful when it's first finished.

Hattie also gave me the most wonderful recipe for quail, which I'd never tasted, but on her instructions I found these little birds, so tiny that they made me feel quite sorry for them.

Quail with Grapes

Buy twice as many quails as you have guests. You can buy very good cans of seedless white grapes, if they are not in season at the time you're cooking the dish. Season the birds and put a rasher of streaky bacon rolled up inside each quail and wrap each one in bacon. Before I actually put then into a casserole I place them under the grill for about 5 minutes, so that the bacon is stuck to them and they're getting a little bit brown looking. Pop them into the casserole surrounded by the seedless grapes (if they're canned, you can put a little of their juice on them). Add a little water and white wine. Put the lid on and cook them in a pre-heated ove of Gas Mark 4/350°F/180°C for 45 minutes.

I was very lucky to do a season in Margate, because Hattie had a house there – a beautiful square-looking house on the front. She visited my caravan very frequently with John and the two children, Robin and Kim. They were very young then, as they were born during 'Educating Archie'. Thinking back on those days has brought to mind something I cooked for her which she rather liked – when I started on this chapter all I could remember were Hattie's lovely dishes, but now the **Prawn Curry** that I did has come back to mind:

Prawn Curry

You need: one chopped onion; 1 crushed garlic clove; a little fat for frying; 1 dessertspoon curry powder; I dessertspoon tomato purée; ground almonds to taste and ½ pint fish stock (I'm not very fond of this, so I use water, but, if you like fish stock – great). You also need: chopped pineapple (canned); 1 chopped red pepper; 1 bunch chopped spring onions and last of all 8 oz prawns.

Fry the chopped onions and crushed garlic in a little fat and when the onions have gone translucent, add the curry powder and tomato purée. Go on frying them together until they have all taken on each other's colour and are beginning to look like an exciting mixture and have a good smell. I don't actually measure the ground almonds but sprinkle about 1 dessertspoon over the top and push them into the mixture until it looks a beautiful reddy-brown colour, but slightly paler because of the almonds. Add the water or stock and cook for about ¾ hour. Then add the pineapple (but not the juice), the pepper and the spring onions – they will need very little cooking, as they should be crunchy. Finally add the prawns and cook for about 3 minutes; they will already be cooked and just need heating through.

If you want to garnish with some chopped parsley it will enhance the look. The taste is absolutely stunning.

61

My caravan at Margate was just like having a tiny home of my own and my brother, his wife Pat and his son and daughter Peter and Susan came and stayed in a little hotel just in front of where my caravan was. They always came to me for lunch. I thought nothing of cooking a couple of ducks and roast potatoes and all that sort of thing in that tiny oven – I don't think much of it now! I'm quite a success with cooking duck and I find that in restaurants they never cook it for long enough.

Pricked Stuffed Duck with Orange

The way I do this is to cut up some peeled oranges into chunks – enough to stuff the duck to make it look bigger than it did when it came from the butcher's. You'll need plenty of oranges so make sure you buy enough. Then I prick it all over with a fork, as though I really hate it (I don't really, because I look forward to enjoying it very much). Then I rub a great deal of salt all over the skin before roasting it on a trivet (or whatever is handy to act as a trivet; the little wire stand that goes under the grill will do) so that the fat will run off the duck, and there's tons of it to come out.

Duck always takes much longer to cook than you imagine: I start it off very high, say Gas Mark 8/475°F/240°C for about 20–30 minutes so that the skins are beginning to get coloured, and then attack it again viciously with a fork – this is a great fight that goes on in the kitchen! – put a bit more salt on and put it back in the oven Gas Mark 6/400°F/200°C. Never cook duck in a low oven as you have to get all the fat out of the skin to have a really beautiful duck, and the heat must stay fairly high for this to happen. When no more fat is coming out, the duck is done. It may take 2 hours for a 5 lb duck to be properly cooked.

I think that you can't carve a duck: I use the secateurs I use for pruning the roses to cut through the breast bone – the bird will be so well cooked it will go straight through and you can cut round just above the legs, so you've got a sort of cross shape on the top. Turn it over and cut it straight down the back, so you've got four separate sections of duck with bone in. I can't stand that sloppy skin that comes with restaurant duck – that's not for me at all.

A carefree caravan moment.

With duck I usually serve **Belgian Red Cabbage** which I'm awfully fond of, and which is practically a meal in itself:

Belgian Red Cabbage

This is a fresh red cabbage, cut up and shredded finely, as finely as you can. Don't put in any of the really thick pieces that look white when you cut through them, because those really won't cook in time. Take out the core and use the cabbage leaves, because they certainly cook and are absolutely beautiful. Finely chop an onion and a cooking apple, which doesn't have to be chopped so finely, because it takes much less time to cook. First of all you fry the onion in butter or margarine or whatever. Then when it's beginning to go transparent, add the red cabbage. Keep turning this over and make sure that it's beginning to cook. It will lose a great deal in bulk in this process, but you're also sweating out a great deal of the juice. Last of all you add the cooking apple and mix well together. Then, when you think they're all cooking, but not sticking to the bottom of the saucepan, you pour in any old red wine you may have handy, or, indeed a bottle of red wine that you don't care about (any old plonk will do). This sloshes over the apple and the red cabbage and the onion. Add salt and pepper, brown sugar and a bay leaf: it is a lovely taste with something like duck and the colour contrasts well so that it looks very pretty when you serve it.

Another dish which goes very well with the duck is:

Potatoes with Chopped Chives

For speed get a can of potatoes and drain off the liquid. Fry with chopped chives, black pepper and salt until they're really brown. This is a recipe for speed, perhaps not so much for quality, but I like it very much, particularly with duck, because the duck, the cabbage and the potatoes are all entirely different tastes. You could have roast potatoes of course. I hope you'll like this recipe.

HALF A KILO OF DONKEY

Now that we're on the move and getting 'international' I feel that I must hark back to the days that I had with my husband Derek Franklin – he too was quite happy with caravan life when we used to do 'Music for the Millions' for Harold Fielding all over the country. During the war he was stationed in Austria, and, of course, unlike me, who'll try any old language and I don't care if I do make a fool of myself, he was much more proud and not so ready to rush in where angels fear to tread when it came to the language barrier. When I was in Spain I asked for 'Una medio kilo de burro' which I found out meant donkey, when what I was trying to ask for was butter, which is *mantequilla*. Everybody in the shop laughed.

AUSTRIA AND THE OSTRICH

We used to go to the Lake District of Austria, which he knew best, for lovely holidays and I must say it was a perfect part of the country, I thought. The Austrian people were so nice, though their cooking seems to me to be slightly limited – they have an awful lot of veal. However there was one thing I had there which I'd never had before and that was **Wienerschnitzel Cordon Bleu**. This was a huge piece of veal escalope, with a sort of pocket cut in the middle of it containing a slice of cheese and a slice of ham. The outside of the pocket was sort of pinned together and they then proceeded to grill or fry it, whichever you wanted. It was wonderful and a lovely taste, but a bit over-much for me. It was like one of those huge T-Bone steaks that I can hardly look at: I'm such a hypocrite, because that really looks like a chunk of animal to me.

Talking of being over-faced, I remember when my nephew, Peter stayed with me back in England (I think he was about seventeen and thought he was frightfully grown-up) and had rather a lot of drink before he went to a very old pub here called the Ostrich. It was an old coaching inn and they used to have one of those Sweeny Todd beds: when they'd got the travellers well and truly drunk they used to pull the lever and the bed used to tip the traveller into the cellar, where he was done away with, robbed and never heard of again. The Ostrich is in Colnbrook, a very old village near my house and, incidentally, the bricks that Honeypot Cottage is built with are seventeenth-century bricks from Colnbrook.

The Ostrich was wonderful: they had about eighty-four varieties of cheese, thirty-four different brands of whisky – it was amazing, but I haven't been there for some time, so I don't know if it's like that now. I suggested going out to the Ostrich for supper to Peter, who was high as a kite, he replied, 'Oh, smashing Beryl,' so we went off to Colnbrook. 'Now, what would you like to eat, Peter?'

The houseboat 'Restful', my guestroom, which gave so many friends so much pleasure.

I asked him when we arrived. 'Oh, a T-Bone Steak!' he said with great enthusiasm. He wasn't looking awfully well at that moment, and when the T-Bone steak arrived he looked at it and suddenly he went a very strange shade of green 'I don't feel awfully well, Beryl!' he said. I told him to go off and do what he had to do – which was quite obvious to me – and that I would take the steak home in a catty-bag. The cats (I can't remember how many there were, because that was quite a while ago now) had rather a nice supper too. At that time, as far as I knew, the bed was not in use, nor, I am assured, is it in working order now!

I've rather digressed, Marlene-wise, as is one of my little ways, from Austria (it's all the fault of the Wienerschnitzel) but Derek and I did go to Vienna, where we sort of finished the holiday off. We went to the State Opera House, which had been rebuilt after it was bombed during the war in exactly the same style as before, and we saw 'Aida'. I'm not an opera buff at all, but I thought it was absolutely beautiful: the staging of it and the sound coming from the orchestra pit was something that really had to be heard and seen to be believed. There were some Americans sitting behind us – three of them, in fact – and we overheard them saying, 'We were in London, England, yesterday, and the day before we did Paris. We went to Westminster Abbey – oh, that really is something, but if you want a really cute little Cathedral – Canterbury!' We were hysterical by this time. We were in a hotel for a few nights and the breakfast was a delight. Though it was **Bacon and Eggs** it was done in a rather different way. They obviously grilled the streaky bacon until it was very crispy, then they made an omelette in a pan – I don't know how many eggs, perhaps two for one and person and three for two. Before it was actually set they put all these beautiful strips of crispy bacon in it and then brought the pan to the table and cut the omelette in half. That, I thought, was a wonderful way to eat bacon and eggs. I do it here sometimes and everybody seems to enjoy it.

Austrian Veal Escalope is a favourite there, and I do it at home, with, of course the English veal I always insist on:

Austrian Veal Escalope	*This is veal escalope beaten up very thin, dipped in egg and bread-crumbs, fried very lightly with a little lemon juice, squeezed on it. Serve it, well seasoned with salt and pepper, with some quartered lemons. This has to be very thin veal indeed – I usually get the butcher to attack it first, then I have another bash with my meat hammer when I get it home – thereby getting rid of all my frustrations!*

65

From the Austrian Lake District we went over the Border into Italy at Merano where I got my first pair of those very pointed shoes in very pale beige suede, with what I call lavatory heels (those rather shaped, not terribly high heels). I'd seen Consuela Semprini wear them and thought they were very elegant, and they did become extremely fashionable in England. I suppose winklepickers were what you called them. We didn't quite know where to go to eat in this small Italian town and Derek went up to a fellow who was sweeping the road and said to him in his best Austrian – as it was just across the Border I suppose they all understood – 'Could you tell us a place to eat?' He threw his shovel and his brush over his shoulder, said, 'Kommen Sie mit mir' and led us to this restaurant nearby and ordered for three, putting up three fingers, so there could be no doubt in anybody's mind that he had joined the party! He ordered some wine and **Italian Calves' Liver**:

Italian Calves' Liver

The Italians do it a very nice way, so it was absolutely beautiful. They fry chopped onions in butter or margarine until they're practically done and then cut the liver into weeny little thin strips, almost like match-sticks, so you lose all the funny bits like little tubes and things that you find in the middle of it. I do this now with scissors. They move the onions when done to the back of the pan and the little bit of fat that's on them will float forward and you drop the liver in that (some people dip the liver in flour but I don't like this because I prefer the gravy not to be thick). Fry the liver with black pepper and salt and it's done in about 4 minutes, because the strips of liver are so thin. Then you serve it on that beautiful bed of onions. Of course, because it's me and I don't like fat, I 'blot' it with kitchen paper, because I can't eat fat. People who don't have that problem will relish the onions served straight from the pan with the liver on top. This is a smashing way to eat liver.

BILTONG AND MANGOES

We're jetting to another continent now and South Africa looms on the horizon. I've described the breath-taking beauty of the country before and the great hospitality I enjoyed from the company I was with in the revue 'Something New'. That was in 1961, and it was a great time of learning about different foods and different tastes for me. The climate is so wonderful, and I couldn't get over the fact that there was a lot of food sold on the side of the road, like Biltong which was an acquired taste; I didn't know whether I liked it or not at first. It's pressed dried beef, which they make into a sort of sausage and it hangs on barrows at the roadside, I grew to like it after a bit. Also on the barrow were mangoes, water melons and sweetcorn which you could buy in those days for practically nothing. I think a mango must have cost about sixpence (about two and a half pence today) and they were so beautiful to eat. I tasted canned mangoes when I was taken to an Indian restaurant when I was very young and they were served as the pudding. I fell in love with the taste of them – it was like a cross between peaches and pineapple – but, of course, when I tasted the fresh ones that was a different thing altogether. Mangoes are something I've since learned to cut in a presentable way to give people here. The trick is to slice down each side of the stone with a knife and then cut the huge stone out. Then make cuts through the flesh but not the skin, first across the shortest way and then lengthways. Finally you can turn the whole thing inside out and it looks like a very beautiful edible porcupine or hedgehog – whichever your taste would be! You can then slice off the little squares with a knife. Apart from getting the stone out, they're fairly easy to prepare. Anyway, I didn't know this trick in Africa and I just used to sit chewing them and taking the peel off as I went.

South Africa was really amazing in that there was so much food to be had from the land, and at such very little cost. My time there was made so happy by the people in the show, who mainly came from England, though my co-star John Boulter was South African; they were absolutely marvellous to me, because I was in another country. I realize now that when I did 'Gigi', Jean-Pierre Aumont, who played the part that Maurice Chevalier did in the film, must have been lonely over here. I rather regret that I didn't think of this earlier, as I could have done more to entertain him. He must really have been a stranger in England, though he made a film here years ago. He was a charming Frenchman and it must have been pretty tough – it is, if you're not in your own country, and particularly if you're very quiet, which he was. I'm pretty gregarious, so I sometimes get better treats than most!

When we went back to Johannesburg after playing in Cape Town I did spend a lot of weekends with John Boulter, whose house reminded me very much of home, because it had round thatched rooms like mine at Honeypot, only much larger. In Africa they're called rondavels. He entertained a good deal and had about five servants – everybody did, but the standard of wages was sadly low and made for what I thought was a pretty rotten life. One of the servants was a wonderful woman of tremendous natural dignity. To see Letty walk was a joy, because everything was carried on her head, and sometimes she was stripped to the waist – we were in the country, though it was so near Johannesburg. Letty was an awfully good cook, and one recipe I had from her, although I have mentioned it before when I told my life story, is so good it bears repeating.

Letty's Fish Pie!   *You steam or simmer as much white fish as you want with some slices of onion. If you were going to play loaves and fishes it could be a substantial amount: when you hear the recipe you'll know how it works out. Flake it and put it into a casserole dish. Then put a layer of tomatoes, a layer of grated lemon rind, one of grated cheese, then one of chopped hard-boiled eggs. I usually put a layer of the cooked onions on mine. Repeat the layers all the way up the dish, then pour white sauce over it and cook it in the oven, I would say slowly at Gas Mark 2/300°F/150°C for about ¾ hour. If you want you can put mashed potatoes on the top, and if you paint them with a little beaten up egg, you will have a beautiful brown top. This isn't really necessary, because the fish pie itself is absolutely delicious.*

During my first visit to New York in 1966 to repeat the part I had played in London in 'The Killing of Sister George' it took some time to find myself an apartment, but I had to do it if I was going to be able to settle down at all in America. It has been said that I'm only happy when buying food and cooking it and never, for any length of time, in hotels. That is the truth, the whole truth and nothing but the truth.

When after a long search I did find my own apartment it was at West 72nd Street: Central Park was at one end and Columbus Avenue at the other end – the wonderful shopping area where all the Puerto Rican people buy their food. Then, if you walked one more block you were back on Broadway. I was in an apartment hotel, which we don't seem to have here, which included maid service. This meant it got vaguely cleaned every day and you had cooking facilities. I had a bedroom, a bathroom, a sitting room and it was really everything that I needed.

I was absolutely in my element in my apartment, although I must say I felt rather silly, because, as you know, Americans have absolutely everything at their fingertips and I'd taken the trouble to pack my beloved garlic crusher, besides all my little other gadgets from the kitchen. I even took

At it again, Eileen and myself.

things like washing powder – I don't know what I thought I was doing, but I always think I'm going to an island, where nobody's ever got anything: it was like Desert Island Discs in New York! It was lovely to be in an apartment and have a few implements to cook with. I settled down immediately and became almost sane again, though I must say I was very lonely in New York. The play only had four women in it and we had all day free, with not a cat in sight! I'd done all the art galleries by this time, so I was delighted when Eileen Atkins moved in four floors above me. I told her, 'Eileen, if you ever want to come to lunch I'll be eating lunch every day.' I knew that at that time she hadn't got a lot of use for cooking, and I try to make lunch my main meal, which is the thing that, for the moment, keeps my weight at bay. I find it very difficult to eat late at night, and practically impossible to eat after a show is over, which, though I've been in the theatre for so long, a great number of my friends find difficult to understand. But your digestion really packs up at half past seven and anything you eat after that is going to lie like a brick on your stomach and not be properly digested at all.

Right bang next door to the apartment block was a supermarket which had all the easy things to take away. I must say I don't use convenience

69

foods unless I absolutely have to. When you read what's on the label it sounds *magical*, and when you eat it it tastes like *rubbish*! It seemed to me that in New York the gentle art of entertaining and cooking for people was totally non-existent; everything was just brought in from shops. If I walked a little further along from the supermarket I came to the fish shop, where ladies could be heard saying, '*Could* you ask the *boy* to bring a *sturgeon* round tonight; were having *company*!' The 'boy' could be anything up to eighty, as long as he'd got a bicycle, and a sort of metal rack in the front with a basket to carry the sturgeon round.

I'm absolutely horrified at the amount of junk food that Americans eat and how it's caught on here. I was taken to a very grand restaurant called The Four Seasons and when I said I'd like a steak I was given a T-Bone with a sauce full of chopped-up pickled onions (how the Dadda would have enjoyed that!) Obviously the steak had been dead for a hundred years and deep *deep* frozen: it had absolutely no taste at all, so I suppose the pickled onions were intended to jazz it up a bit. But they certainly didn't do anything for me.

Anyway I would ring Eileen Atkins or she would ring me and she'd come down often. One thing I remember that Eileen liked very much was a particular chicken dish, although she doesn't like anything that looks like a bird. My favourite butcher, Harold (who was such a whizz at cutting chickens and did it so automatically and so quickly you would have to jump in quick and say, '*Don't* cut it up!' if you didn't want it dismembered) came into his own then, as it were, by cutting all the chicken meat off the bones for me. I used the bones separately, because they do give the stock a bit of substance. This is the recipe for Eileen's Non-Chicken Dish!

Chicken Creole

Have a chicken cut into joints, or buy chicken joints and skin them – I make no bones (no pun intended, but you may smile if you wish!) about repeating that I always skin them, because there is too much fat in the skin for me to make any dish palatable. Fry the joints in butter or whatever and herbs, remove them from the pan and put them into a casserole.

In a little cup or dish mix 1 teaspoon ground ginger, 1 teaspoon ground coriander, and one each of mixed spice and of nutmeg and 1 dessertspoon plain flour. When you mix all these together it's a beautiful sort of plain brown powder, which smells lovely. Then you see what you've got left in the saucepan, which will be a few mixed herbs and perhaps a little of the butter or margarine. Add a bit more of both. Pour the mixed spices into the fat and make it into a roux. By now it's beginning to smell wonderful. In the original recipe you add the juice of 6 oranges, but that becomes rather expensive now, so I use a can of unsweetened orange juice and I put enough of this into this roux to make it into a really nice thick sauce, very orangey. The smell quite bowls you over – a lot of the pleasure of cooking is enjoying it as you go. When the sauce looks absolutely smooth and hand-some pour it over the top of the chicken joints. Then cook gently in a moderately hot oven at Gas Mark 5/375°F/190°C for between ¾–1 hour, until the chicken is tender.

I serve this with **Boiled Rice.** *I boil it first, then when it has come to the boil, run it under the cold water, in a sieve. I put the sieve over a pan with water in it and put the lid on top, so that in fact the rice steams itself into separate grains, and becomes all individual and nice. The rice doesn't need any colouring – it's white rice, which looks quite attractive. I serve the chicken with the same sort of bits that I would with curry, as it's a Creole dish: sweet mango chutney; lime pickle; may be very finely chopped onion with mint, covered with lemon juice; sliced bananas also sprinkled with lemon juice, just to keep them from losing their colour; and perhaps a little yoghurt – anything that you would serve with an Indian meal.*

One of the things I ate in America, which was so simple and absolutely lovely was **Cinnamon Toast,** which they usually eat at breakfast, but you can have with any meal – it really doesn't matter:

Cinnamon Toast   *Cut the crusts off slices of bread. They can be white or brown, according to taste. Beat up an egg, really quite savagely, until it's well mixed. Paint the bread with the egg and add a little ground cinnamon to each side. Fry this, and the end result really is a glorious taste. I think it was one of the easy things I liked best. You can have it with sugar if you want.*

7
Cooking with Love

When I first moved to Honeypot Cottage from the caravan I was living in between Windsor and Maidenhead, it was love at first sight. The people who lived here loved it so little that they'd pinned navy blue velvet over the glass door that looked onto the river and they thought I was raving mad when I said, 'Oh, how wonderful!' They hated the river and nobody could grow a flower here, because the trees hadn't been cut back. When I looked in the kitchen there was a cooker on bricks and a sink on bricks; there was wet rot in the kitchen and dry rot in the bedroom. None of this was going to dampen my enthusiasm; you see I could imagine exactly what it was going to look like and the colours and everything – the olive greens and the oranges and those sort of things that were going to feature in the living room. If you can see in your mind's eye what a place is going to look like in the end, then you're a lucky person, and I was at that time. The kitchen now is quite another story: funnily enough, having lived in a caravan helped me very much to re-design the kitchen from the point of view of size or lack of it. I had a wonderful man called Mr. Gibson, who, of course is retired now and I showed him what sort of shape I would like the cupboards to be in the kitchen. Because it is round it's difficult to find things to fit, but I have found room for a rather beautiful and very nice cooker. I still cook by calor gas, because I really don't like cooking by electricity and there is no gas in Wraysbury. So I have gas cylinders in a box just outside the wall of the kitchen and it's piped in – a bit like the haggis! I think this is a wonderful way to cook; the only boring thing about it is the cylinders give no indication when they're going to run out. I now have two adjoining cylinders with a little switch-over gadget – you just change the hose lead with a turn of the hand and put it on the other cylinder.

A BOAT TRIP ON THE THAMES

I remember once when Lord and Lady Craigton, Eileen and Jack, and Norman Newell came round and I'd really knocked my soul case out doing two pheasants. I'd got them wrapped up in bacon and I'd got a piece of celery and a piece of fat bacon rolled up inside and had stuffed them with bread soaked in port wine. I'd fried the breadcrumbs and I'd got the redcurrant jelly and the game chips. Everything was ready when they arrived, but Jack Craigton suddenly said, 'I can't smell any cooking'. 'Neither can I,' I cried. Of course the gas cylinder was a faulty one – it had conked out, which was very unfortunate, and I started to cry. 'Don't worry,' said Eileen, 'Don't bother at all; we'll just lift it all into the boot of our car!' and we just had to do that. It was a terrible come-down for me and I was very upset about it. So it was all cooked at the Craigtons', instead of having lunch here. The wine and everything was transported to their house, and we had it there. I felt a bit of a nana, but it didn't seem to matter to anybody else but me; that was just because I'd planned it as one of the best meals they'd ever had and I was going to be the proud dirty waitress, and I'd failed slightly miserably! If you're kind of a brave cook you must never

be upset by the terrible things that happen occasionally on the way – just rub it out, take a deep breath, dust yourself off and start all over again.

Eileen and Jack entertain me frequently in their house and the biggest treat is that they have a piece of beautiful beef which has the fillet on one side and the superlative beef on the other, delivered from Scotland, every fortnight I think. I believe it's about £20 in money and a great deal in weight and it is magnificent – it just melts in your mouth and Eileen cooks it like an angel. She sometimes goes so far as to make Yorkshire pudding, but I think Jack has to give her money for that, because he loves Yorkshire pudding and I don't think she feels like fiddling with it after cooking the beef. Of course, when she does make it it's wonderful too. I don't see them nearly as often as I'd like to, or even talk to them as often as I'd like to, because they're very near me on the river. Jack is in the House of Lords and I'm busy, and this is the way of things with the friends I have: we just get together the best way we can, but when we do it's always a kind of celebration. They have been absolutely marvellous to me; they've two smashing boats – I think Lacewing is the one we usually go out in – and sometimes if it's a lovely day they take me up the river because I haven't got a boat of my own and I say, 'Oh, this will have to be my summer holidays!' It's a great joy to have lunch there and get on board the boat with whatever drinks we're drinking beside us. They're very game and care-free – Eileen is extremely funny and never fails to make me laugh. We have got a lot going for us as a little trio of friends.

I digress here for a moment, because my cat Elsie – she who had such an unhappy beginning in Bristol and has turned into such a happy and funny cat – has gone a little bit crackers for the moment and has taken it into her head to take swipes at the chord attached to the tape recorder, while Dimly and Jenny are stretched out relaxed on the 'office bed' and taking absolutely no notice of such prankish goings on. Strangely enough their presence is not only soothing – it actually helps the flow of consciousness when you're trying to remember.

JOAN BISSETT AND THE SURPRISE BIRTHDAY LUNCH

I remember so well and with such great affection my friend Joan Bissett, who came here to help me for twenty years. Very sadly, I went away to do 'Romeo and Juliet' for the National Theatre in 1974 at the Harrogate Festival. I was only away for three days and Joan died in those three days. As she always sort of depended on me to help her with her health because I happened to know a lot of good people at that time (and still do, thank goodness), she didn't know where to look for help and she died of a perforated intestine before she was fifty years old. We had so many happy years together and I still imagine she's always about the place somehow: she was lovely and didn't expect any surprises at all. I used to round up her three daughters secretly when her birthday came round and I told her some long-winded story about how my director friend Freddie Carpenter was coming to lunch. During the morning of Joan's birthday I said, 'You'd better polish the glasses, Joan.', to get her out of the kitchen, so she couldn't see what I was doing. Actually I was going to do for starters something terribly easy which is good when you've got a busy day. It was **Taramasalata**, for which I've got a lovely recipe:

Taramasalata   *For four people, you need: an 8 oz packet of cream cheese (Demi Sel, or something like that); a smoked cod's roe and ½ oz butter or whathaveyou. Cream the cheese, the roe and the butter in a basin. Then add lemon juice, cayenne pepper, a skinned and crushed garlic clove and a little brandy. You mix them all together and it comes out a beautiful pink colour. Put it into little dishes, with perhaps a black olive and some parsley sticking out of the top and pop it into the fridge. This is a wonderful first course, with a bit of dry toast and of course a fish fork to cope with it.*

Her next course was going to be **Tournedos Rossini**, which I seldom do now, because fillet steak is very expensive:

Tournedos Rossini *For each person you need one tiny, rather thick, perfect round of fillet steak with no fat on the outside. In the meantime fry some rounds of bread, cut to fit the steaks in whatever meat fat you have, such as dripping. Cut some rounds of paté to fit the steaks. You can buy this and there are several kinds available that are quite acceptable, provided you know what you're eating. Keep the bread hot, but of course the paté mustn't get too hot or it disintegrates entirely. Grill the steaks with black pepper – a lot of black pepper – on each side. I like them medium rare, but you have to trust your own judgement in this case. I also like to put a couple of little fillets of anchovy out of a can on the top. I usually serve them with new potatoes, if they're in season (if not, maybe croquettes) and spinach is awfully nice with what is quite a rich dish. My spinach just grows happily among the flowers here and*

75

comes up year after year. It was given to me by Eileen Craigton in the first place. Purple flowering broccoli, if it's in, would be nice with it, or you might just care for a tossed green salad.

For Joan's pudding I made one of my favourites, **Treacle Tart**. It was really rather selfish, of me, but I love it and so, I think did she. I know it's death to your waist line, but just for the moment I throw my bonnet to the windmill and I just don't care.

Joan's Treacle Tart

You start off by making 6 oz shortcrust pastry. Add a beaten egg to the pastry mix before making up the liquid with water. This was my brother Roy's idea or invention, because he was a research chemist and did research on high explosives, make-up – you name it; he did it. He also did research on food, and we found out that an egg in the pastry does make a tremendous amount of difference to it. Roll out the dough to fit a flan tin or dish 6 inches in diameter. Sometimes I use a tin with a metal handle on its edge but it also goes under the tart you're making. If the pastry sticks a bit you can whizz it round to get it loose. Bake the pastry blind for about 15–20 minutes in a moderate oven at Gas Mark 6/400°F/200°C. Prick the pastry too, and put a bundle of beans upon it in grease-proof paper – whatever you want to keep it flat. When it's really set, you take it out and let it cool.

In the meantime, mix the grated rind of a lemon and 3 tablespoons golden syrup and enough breadcrumbs – I use brown breadcrumbs for this – to really give it a proper feeling of being solid when you cut it. If there's too much syrup it gets sloppy. (If it looks too sloppy keep filling it up as it's cooking with the brown breadcrumbs). Put it back into the oven and cook it for 15–20 minutes while the magical performance of the breadcrumbs blending into the syrup goes on. When you think it's right and when you think it's cooked you take it out, let it cool, or you can serve it hot. Personally I think it's better cool. If you're going to put cream on it, which we did that day (we were going raving mad!) it's nicer when it's cool. Some people put cornflakes, or even rice crispies in it, but I've never done this.

That really was a smashing lunch. Of course, Freddie Carpenter wasn't coming and Joan had been polishing the glasses, not exactly in vain, because

76

we were going to use them. When it was time for her to go home she went to the door and there were her three daughters standing there. 'What are you lot doing here?' she said. 'Joan Bisset, This is Your Birthday!' I cried. We then celebrated with a bottle of Toff's Lemonade, or, as others might prefer to call it Charlie Goldtop. It just means champagne, which is pretty good by any name. I know Peter Graves always used to call it Charlie Goldtop, and since then I have taken to calling it Toff's Lemonade. Whatever we called it, it put the seal on a really lovely affair.

JIMMY EDWARDS AND THE CURRY

When Jimmy Edwards was married and we worked together an awful lot I was playing Brighton and he and his wife, Valerie, lived in Sussex. They invited me to lunch and she cooked a most wonderful curry. I have a kind of foolproof recipe for curry, but she had done something I didn't know about, which was to add pinenuts to it, and it's lovely, because it adds a bit of crunch in the middle of the curry.

Curry

You need: 2 large onions – I like to use Spanish onions, because they're not quite so lethal; 2 garlic cloves; 1½ lb very lean pork, diced, or very lean beef, similarly cut into cubes; about 2½ tablespoons curry powder; a small can of tomatoes; ½ pint stock; 1 teaspoon ground ginger; 1 teaspoon coriander seeds; 4 cloves; 1 inch of cinnamon stick; 1 teaspoon cumin seeds; 2 chopped dried chillies; a little dash of chilli sauce; a little soy sauce; ½ a lemon, chopped with the rind on; 1 oz ground almonds and 1 dessertspoon pinenuts.

Start off by chopping the onions, crushing the garlic and putting them in the frying pan. Let them cook together in the fat of your choice until the onion is transparent. Then add the chopped up meat and stir until it is sealed. Then add the curry powder until the meat really gets the curry cooked into it. Add the tomatoes, nicely chopped up, and the stock (cubes, if you haven't got your own stock pot) but this is all going to get used up, so you do have to watch it. Next, add the rest of the ingredients except the almonds and pinenuts. Let this cook and keep checking the liquid level, for about 1 hour. This

Me and big Jim, tucking in.

77

seems rather long, but you'll be so riveted by the smell of it that you won't care; you'll be intoxicated by the different fumes – perhaps aromas is a more suitable word. Then you add the ground almonds, which take up a great deal of the liquid, but they do give it a wonderful taste. At the same time, if you can get pinenuts – they are rather expensive – just put about a dessertspoonful into the curry and this gives it a lovely texture.

I don't know how the Indians make the rice that you have in Indian restaurants taste so marvellous – it has that delicate kind of scented smell and a beautiful colour. I just do the rice 'My Way', as I have described on page 71.

That was my glorious meal with Jimmy Edwards and I've repeated the recipe here – I couldn't count the number of times. It's *really* scrumptious: just the smell is a feast in itself – you don't actually need to eat it – the smell is almost enough.

A NIGHT OUT WITH JOHN LE MESURIER

When I was in Margate, and at one time I always seemed to be playing there – Hattie Jacques was away, and John Le Mesurier who was always hanging around spare when she wasn't there (he was so delightfully vague) asked me, 'I wonder if you'd like to have a little meal after the performance tonight'. 'Oh, John, I'd love to', I replied. He was always such an entertaining person and so funny in that dry way of his. I asked him if he knew anywhere we could go and he said, 'Well, there's a sort of café place along the front. So, as it wasn't far from the theatre, we padded the hoof along to this 'café place', which was really quite nice, except there was a huge glass window in the front so that you could look in and see everybody eating in there and what they were eating and they could look out at you – like a large marine goldfish bowl. It was licensed, which appealed to both of us, so we went in. It was an Italian-type restaurant, so we probably had tagliatelli verde or chicken livers on rice topped with grated cheese, but we didn't get any further, because there was a young man who had had an awful lot to drink sitting at the next table and the tables were quite close. Suddenly he rushed out of the restaurant, stood in front of this glass window and was sick all over the place. 'Oh well', said John, 'He's had his main course – he'll be ready for the pudding now!'

Years later, when John was married to Joan we were making a film together at Swanage and they took me out twice to wonderful suppers to a restaurant where all the crew used to go. I'm happy to say we were always able to get through the whole meal, as the incident was never repeated! You know that if the crew are to be found eating in a restaurant it's rather like going into a restaurant abroad where the locals are eating. You know its going to be all right. If the crew go there it's got to be the best food they've found in the vicinity.

Although we were in the same hotel we had no communicating phones and there was only one telephone box in the hotel, so I couldn't ring them up. When I came home and had had a bath, I used to rush up to their room about three floors above me, knock at the door and say 'Are you all right: can I bring my drink in and have one with you?' You see, I had my brandy with me and they were on vodka and tonic. So, of course, that's what we used to do every evening. Then one weekend I thought I must find something absolutely lovely to do with them. We ended up at a quite exceptional fish restaurant in Lulworth Cove where I was able to repay John and Joan's hospitality and, may I say, a good time was had by all. In fact, it was quite a story in itself as I have related, as the Americans love to say 'in depth', elsewhere.

ROY PLOMLEY AND 'FAVOURITE THINGS'

Roy Plomley was another lovely person who came to my house when we were doing his television programme 'Favourite Things'. He was such a great person and yet the extraordinary thing was he seemed to draw everything out of you – you couldn't help talking, although he wasn't really asking questions; I could never fathom this great trick he had. He was married to a Chinese lady who was obviously a wonderful cook.

I had them all – that is, Roy Plomley, the director Michael Kerr and both their secretaries to meals at Honeypot, which was really the theme of the programme. The crew used to go to a pub in the village and have some food, because I couldn't cook for a crew of seven as well. I did the cooking while they were changing the lighting round. The cats were at first wary and a bit resentful while all this was going on, but when they got used to the people and the activity their natural gregariousness asserted itself – curiosity got the better of them and they joined in the action when the spirit moved them.

If we were going to have something that had to cook for a long time, I used to prepare it when they'd gone during the evening and cook it that night, or start the cooking that night and leave it cooking all the following morning, if it was that sort of a dish. Roy Plomley *was* that sort of a dish

– I thought he was wonderful and it didn't seem possible when I heard that he had died so soon after we made the programme. He was so vital; you couldn't possibly have guessed that he had anything the matter then, and yet he must have been seriously ill at that time.

Somehow I always managed to produce a meal – I don't quite know how, because we were in the garden, we were all over the place. I cooked kidneys the way that Billy Chappell, of whom you're going to hear more, taught me to cook them. As there was quite a lot of preparation involved this was something I started the previous evening. Here's how I made **Lambs' Kidneys à la Chappell**:

Lambs' Kidneys à la Chappell

You need 1 lb lambs' kidneys, for preference (but if you want to enlarge the bulk you can also add, a veal kidney if there's one going. This is delightful, but, if not, an ox kidney that looks fairly young will be extremely tasty and they're much less expensive than lambs' kidneys). Halve the kidneys, skin and core them and cut them into tiny pieces. This takes quite a while, which is why I started the night before. As there were five of us and I was only giving them one meal a day, and I was only eating one meal a day, I did run to lambs' kidneys, and put the tiny pieces into the fridge overnight. For the cooking I took a large chopped onion in a saucepan, in butter or margarine, and fried it until it was beginning to look beautiful – not brown – just transparent. Then I added the kidneys. Kidneys take an awful long time to cook properly. Billy always says, 'You put in a little bit of this and a little bit of that' and, of course I understand what he means. When the kidneys have gone a pale brown colour you add salt and pepper, a little bit of Lea and Perrins, a little squeeze of tomato purée, which gives it that nice pink colour, a little bit of lemon juice. When you've put in all your little bits of this and little bits of that', you add about ½ pint stock, and let the kidneys and the onion and the rest all cook together very, very gently, just simmering for about 1 hour. Keep checking the level of the liquid, as you've got a saucepan with the lid on. If the liquid has gone down, you might care to add a little old red wine . . .

Eric has just asked, 'What is this Old Red Wine *and how is it you've always got it hanging about?' Well, I usually have, because I always put it in the fridge and the great trick with it is to put a tiny bit of olive oil or whatever oil you use for cooking and let it float on the top of the wine to keep it fairly new and not so old and tatty. It can, of course, be any sort of oil: Corn oil, Flora oil, which I use now for cooking, or even Trex which they now do as a liquid. I remember it in its heyday as something in a tub with which I used to take off my make-up when I first trod, or hoofed, the boards! Time and progress evidently continue to march on. A little bit of any light oil, just floated on the top, will make That Old Black Magic of the Old Red Wine by keeping it fresher than it would otherwise be. That is an old tip from Italy that my friend Reggie Vincent gave me.*

But I've digressed again, as is my wont. To continue the recipe for 'My Favourite Things' – and People lunch (as director Michael Kerr was also a joy to work with) – Just when you feel the kidneys are beginning to be done, you test them with a little knife or fork. Mix two heaped teaspoonfuls of powdered mustard into a saucer with water and you add it all to the kidneys. Then let them continue to cook for another twenty minutes with the mustard. The extraordinary thing is that there is absolutely no taste of mustard in the end result, which I kind of didn't believe at the time.

I prefer to serve the kidneys on rice, but you could do mashed potatoes if you liked. For the benefit of the television cameras we poured some brandy on and set fire to it – but that was really more of a joke for us, it's not necessary. It is nice though to add a little sherry at the end, or a little brandy. If it makes you feel better, you do it: I do!

LUNCH WITH JOHN GIELGUD

When I was in New York doing the play of 'The Killing of Sister George' I quite frequently met John Gielgud; I had met him before but not very often. I've always been in awe of him, like I was of Noel Coward and I think he's the most wonderful very funny man. Of course I did work with him later on in the film of 'Joseph Andrews'. A short time after the film 'George', during 1969, I think it was, he invited me to have lunch with him at his house, which was in a little square facing the river, opposite the Houses of Parliament. I was so over-anxious I got there terribly early. I was ashamed of this, because you don't want everybody to know that you're over-anxious and so I thought I would have a little walk along the Embankment. It was the time when black net stockings with patterns such as flowers on, were frightfully fashionable (like they are now, only these days they're tights). I was wearing these and a black dress with a lot of print tiny red and pink flowers on – it was frightfully pretty, and over this black background I had a little short fur jacket. There I was, walking along the Embankment, and I suddenly found I was being rather picked up by people. I thought however early I was I must escape from this and get to John Gielgud's house, so I crossed over the road from the river side and walked a little quicker, and made my way to his house.

He's a fabulous host, so full of energy and humour, always talking about his next six jobs, because he's always got millions of jobs lined up. The thing that stands out in my mind about the lunch – I think we were six at table, but, apart from John I hadn't met anyone before – was that we had a spectacular pudding. He had a rather old housekeeper, and in those days I wouln't have dared ask how you cooked it, but I've since discovered that it was probably a **Victoria Sponge Pudding** for which I have a recipe:

Victoria Sponge Pudding

The basis was a Victoria Sponge mixture, and as there was quite a big dish of this, you'd need: 6 oz butter; 6 oz caster sugar; 6 oz self-raising flour and 3 eggs. Cream the butter and the sugar. Then add the flour and the eggs alternately – this is where the work comes in, because you've got to 'fold' them in in a figure of eight. Put the mixture into a greased, deep ovenproof dish. Bung it in the middle of the oven at Gas Mark 4/375°F/180°C – I'm getting quite used to that now! What I imagine happened with this was that they took it out after about 35 minutes, just before it was cooked and spread the top of it with mincemeat and just left it for another 10 minutes to cook until the gunge from the mincemeat went into the sponge. Then they poured a couple of glasses of brandy over it. We had this lovely sponge cake with the mincemeat on it and the brandy on top, and, of course, cream, and I thought I was on the Highroad to Heaven!

THE 'GET UP AND GO' TRIO

When I was asked to do the children's programme 'Get Up and Go', in which Mooncat was my great love and Stephen Boxer was my kind-of-lodger, I was tremendously lucky because I met someone who has since become one of my very special friends, Maria Price. She's a designer and was a great friend of the director-producer Lesley Rogers, who has since died, tragically young. Because I was in a bit of a hole she agreed, for that time, not only to design the clothes, but also to be my 'Minder'. She's totally opposite to me, very quiet with a very softly spoken voice – a bit like the Queen! – and is a magnificent cook, full of the most original ideas. At the same time I had an Italian girl called Vivian, who used to come and do my hair at seven o'clock in the morning with steam tongs – she too was full of ideas for food. We were rather a good trio because we would spark each other off.

When I was rather ill recently and not really able to get around the kitchen a lot – I think I'd broken my arm, again – Maria drove up from Brighton (she used to live in Yorkshire, where, of course, we did the Mooncat series) with everything prepared and she'd cooked me this chicken, with mint, yoghurt, light oil and lemon juice. It was shades of Bron's chicken again, and I've kind of dined out on it since, because, once more, it's perfectly simple, but a very unusual taste.

Maria's Chicken

You need: 2 tablespoons light oil (sunflower oil, she suggests, but I would suggest Flora oil or Trex oil or whatever you particularly like); the juice of 1 lemon; 1 teaspoon turmeric; 2–3 tablespoons cumin powder; a large handful of chopped fresh mint or 1 table-spoon dried mint; pepper and a garlic clove. Joint a chicken and skin the joints, because, again I'm back on the fat kick. You also need a 5 oz carton natural yoghurt.

Mix the oil, lemon juice, the spices, the mint, pepper and the crushed garlic clove. Put this in a dish and let the chicken marinate for 1 hour. You can leave it overnight if you're going to cook it the next day. Either keep it in the same dish or move it to another dish that you want to serve it in. Put a lid on it or cover it with foil just as it is, and cook it for $1\frac{1}{4}$–$1\frac{1}{2}$ hours at Gas Mark 4/350°F/ 180°C. When it's cooked, take it out of the oven and mix in the yoghurt with the liquor that you've cooked the chicken in. Serve with either couscous, rice or new potatoes. That's easy enough.

Couscous, for anyone not familiar with it, is like a sort of rice mixture: Maria has sent me her way of preparing it: She says, 'I always buy Cypressa couscous – it seems readily available in Health Food stores and is always stocked in Oriental stores – you know, like the one in Wraysbury! (That's a pun, because Oriental stores are notable by their absence in Wraysbury).

Couscous

Put 1 lb couscous into a pudding basin, just covered with freshly boiled, salted water. Add a knob of butter (or whatever). Leave

Two scenes from 'A Little Bit on the Side'. With Janet Mahoney and Michael Remick.

for 10 minutes until the couscous has soaked up all the water. Place the pudding basin over a saucepan of boiling water to keep warm, or use it immediately. If you prefer, you can toss it in a frying pan with some melted butter which gives it a buttery flavour. Season with salt and pepper.

Maria reminded me that when I was working on the revue 'A Little Bit On The Side' at the Theatre Royal, Brighton, I went to lunch with her and took my friends Jon and Antony and she gave us **Old English Pie**. This is how she made it:

Old English Pie

You need: 6 pieces of chicken, skinned and boned and cut into bite-size pieces; a little flour; oil for sautéeing; 1 pint chicken stock; ½ lb sausagemeat; oregano; thyme; grated lemon rind; salt and pepper; 4 oz mushrooms; 4 oz boiled ham or 4 rashers of bacon; 3 hard-boiled eggs; 1 packet of frozen puff pastry, thawed, and a little single cream.

She dusted the chicken with a little flour and sautéed it until it was golden brown. Then she added ½ pint of the stock and cooked it for 10 minutes to thicken. She went on to mix the sausagemeat with a sprinkling of oregano, thyme, grated lemon rind, salt and pepper. With wet hands she formed the sausagemeat into

84

small balls and sautéed them in a pan. Then she removed them from the pan. Then she sautéed mushrooms and ham or bacon. She cut the hard-boiled eggs into quarters and greased an old -fashioned oval pie dish. She put the chicken pieces in it with some of the gravy and neatly arranged sausagemeat balls evenly around the dish, placing pieces of egg in between. She scattered mushrooms and ham on top. Then she rolled out the pastry, placed a thin strip around the edge of the pie dish and moistened it. She placed the rest of the pastry on top. She fluted the edges into scallops and glazed the top with beaten egg. Then she cooked the pie at Gas Mark 5–6/375–400°F/190–200°C until the pastry had risen and was golden. Finally she made gravy with the remaining stock, added a little single cream and grated lemon rind, salt and pepper to taste. She served it with new potatoes and broccoli or new carrots.

'If They Asked Me I Could Write a Book' full of Maria's recipes, but those samples will have to do for now – Thanks a million, Maria!

Vivian, who did my hair in the Mooncat days, was a very inventive cook, too, and she had a special **Brisket and Vegetables** recipe:

Brisket and Vegetables

Brisket of beef is really a very inexpensive joint, and it's best with a very lean brisket. First select whatever vegetables you think you might like with it; perhaps onions finely sliced, carrots finely sliced, if you like them, also mushrooms, cut up very finely and a crushed garlic clove. You put the meat on top of these vegetables, on a piece of foil, shiny side inside, then put more vegetables on top. You can choose tomatoes, and either the same vegetables as below or any others you fancy that will go with them. Add the other half of the crushed garlic clove. Make this into a very firm, wrapped-up parcel, which you put in an ovenproof dish and cook in the middle of the oven at Gas Mark 3/325°F/170°C and forget about it. If you're going to eat it in the evening it can cook practically all day, because it comes out with a great deal of the juice of the meat and all the vegetable juices. Leave it there, say for $3\frac{1}{2}$–4 hours – as long as you want to leave it there. As it's on such a low heat it really doesn't matter. When you take it out, slice the meat, which is like cutting butter by that time, and lay it on a heated dish, with the vegetables all round the meat, or over the *meat, or even among the meat, as they're all practically liquid by then. Make a sauce of creamed horseradish and soured cream in equal quantities, with a bit of the juice from the vegetables and the meat. Mix that together, while you're keeping the meat and everything warm in that low oven, then you pour this glorious sauce over it, and it's a very inexpensive, but beautiful dinner.*

SHARKEY'S BANGERS

James Sharkey, my agent for the film and 'straight' side of my life – Robert Luff, as you will have gathered, handles the rest – was someone I met in 1955 in the Theatre Royal, Windsor revue 'The World's The Limit'. He was in it and so was the girl who became his wife, Isabel George, as were Peter Graves and Patrick Cargill. He came to eat at Honeypot then and, though we met out for meals in the course of business, there was kind of a gap until this book, when he came to meet the cats and sample the fare of Honeypot again!

In the meantime he did send me two practical and very tasty recipes. The first called Cassolet D'Ingham, which I think is the name of Jimmy's house, but by any other name might be regarded as **Very Superior Bangers and Mash**!:

Very Superior Bangers and Mash

You need: 1 lb thick pork sausages; 1 lb onions; a little fat for frying; 1 can oxtail soup.

Grill or bake the sausages (on a trivet, so the fat runs away) until cooked. At the same time, in a large saucepan, fry the onions in a little fat for about 20 minutes until tender. When the sausages are cooked, cut them into 1 inch pieces, add them to the cooked onions with the soup and heat. Serve with mashed potatoes and green vegetables. Serves 4.

Jimmy's other recipe came from the husband of his aunt Elsa, who passed it on to him.

Apple Danny

You need: 1½ lb cooking apples; 1 oz sugar, or to taste; 2 eggs, separated; 1 lime jelly.

Peel, core and slice the apples and cook in a little water with the sugar until soft. Pulp with a potato masher. When cool, spoon into a serving dish and stir in the beaten egg yolks. Dissolve the jelly in half the water stated on the packet. When cool stir into

86

the apple and egg mixture. Whisk the egg whites until really stiff then gently fold them into the mixture. Put in the fridge to set, preferably overnight. Serves 6.

One marvellous recipe I have found which always worked if I had three or four people to lunch, who perhaps didn't know each other was **Fondue**. It was a great way to *make* the guests talk.

Fondue with Rump Steak

You have to have one of those little bronze fondue saucepans with methylated spirits in the thing underneath. Put some fat – oil this time – in the saucepan and cut the beautiful rump steak into little squares. For four people you would really need $1\frac{1}{2}$–2 pounds of rump steak. First of all you need a rather super salad of any kind to go with it and also because potatoes don't really go with it, a few bowls of crisps sitting round the side.

Then I make these dips: I do a little Curry Sauce, *which you just make up as you go along: fry $\frac{1}{2}$ onion and add some curry paste to it, then a squeeze of lemon juice and some water. When the onion is cooked, just swing it around until it begins to look like sauce. That I put in one little bowl, then I have some* Sweet and Sour Sauce, *which I must admit is usually out of a bottle, because you can't do everything. Then there's some* Green Label Mango Chutney, *chopped up very fine;* Tomato Sauce *mixed with* Chilli Sauce, *which is also a lovely dip;* Horseradish Sauce; Soured Cream with Cucumber *grated into it and lemon juice and black pepper; and then there's* Salsa Verde, *which is capers, parsley, gherkins, garlic and a little mayonnaise mixed together. There's also a sauce I make with mayonnaise, mushrooms that have been fried and chopped up very small.*

So there's a number of little dips and I have some long fondue forks with which they're all busy selecting these little cubes of steak and the greedy ones put two cubes on. They're all saying, 'That's mine, that's mine!' 'No, mine's overdone, mine's over-done!' and dipping their forks in with fierce concentration to cook the meat before plunging it into the dips. I've never known anything in the food line to get people to know each other as quickly as this dish does. It is somehow very filling, as you seem just to go on cooking your own little pieces of steak till you fall back exhausted – not to say sated! Again, I always have something like three pieces of kitchen paper each, so that those who don't want the oil on the meat can 'blot' it on the paper. It's a great thing to get people talking, because they're all fighting over whose fork it is and how long it's been cooking in the fat. All inhibitions fly to the wind. It's really great fun, and if you just give them a cold pudding that's all they can manage.

JUDI DENCH

I'd like to end this chapter, 'Cooking with Love', with a recipe from someone for whom I have a lot of love and a very high regard, Judi Dench. We were together in Congreve's 'The Way of the World' in 1978, when I was Lady Wishfort, who described herself, glancing in her mirror to prepare to make the most of herself for a forthcoming levée before a gentleman caller, as 'an old peeled wall'. Judi played Millamant, and, though the critics still rave about Edith Evans as the 'greatest Millamant ever' – I didn't have the pleasure of seeing her – I'm sure Judi gave her a run for her money. At least, Dorothy Dickson, who was a friend of Dame Edith, said so, when she came to see Judi and myself after the performance.

Judi took the trouble to give me the following recipe at a time when she was not only playing her acclaimed Cleopatra at the Olivier Theatre, but in the throes of two plays for television, Michael Frayn's 'Make and Brake' and the following week, Ibsen's 'Ghosts', no less!

Smoked Kipper Pâté

You need: 2 smoked kippers; 2 teaspoons prepared horseradish (or fresh if available); 1 medium packet of Philadelphia Cream Cheese; a carton of double cream; salt and pepper.

Skin the kipper fillets and flake the flesh in a bowl. Add the horseradish and cream cheese and mix thoroughly, adding enough cream to make a smooth mixture. Add salt and pepper (freshly ground is best) and divide into four ramekins or bowls. Garnish with parsley sprigs or a dusting of paprika and serve with thin toast and quartered lemon.

Judi told me that, having prepared this as a starter for a party, she left the dishes on the table and went to fetch the guests. 'When we returned, she says, 'we found every ramekin completely cleaned out and four very contented cats washing their faces!' Meet Tabbsy, Fossil, Spider and Newps.

She's not only a lovely person and a great actress, but a cat lover as well – how many blessings can one person possess?

8
My Favourite Things
Food Shops, Markets, Restaurants and Picnics

Do you know, I really rather hate shopping for clothes, because I get quite desperate if I can't immediately see what I want to wear: even today I have had to force myself to buy three new pairs of shoes, you see I never do it one at a time – I always get three or four pairs at a time, so I don't have to go back!

On the other hand, one of my favourite things is shopping for food: this affords me the greatest satisfaction and I stand there gazing in rapture – it's a bit obscene, I suppose, but never mind. There's one glorious fish shop in Chiswick, called Portch. The fourth generation of the family own it now. The great-grandfather opened it – the establishment celebrates the first hundred years of Portch this year – then his grandfather ran it, now 'Father Bear', Mr. Brian Portch is there and his son is also in the business, so that makes four generations.

Father Portch – the one I know quite well – makes it such a pleasure to shop there, because he has the most wonderful selection of all kinds of fish and I have to ask what everything is, if I don't know. I was talking about the oriental dish with round fish a while ago in this book – well, he's got lots of little round fishes with fat tummies; I don't know what half of them are. Of course, as it is a fish *and* poultry shop you can buy quail and pigeon. I would really like to know what you can't buy there. You can get guinea fowl, which I love, and boiling fowls, very cheaply. You can also buy oysters, clams (tiny little clams and great big ones) and salmon galore for not much money. You can buy caviar, beautiful finnan haddocks – all the sort of things that you dream about; tiny little whitebait, and sprats, which I have never eaten (I'm like Jack Sprat, who could eat no fat and his wife could eat no lean), and also the kind of sardines you get in Spain, with all the coarse sea salt. Sardines Espagnoles are done by

I think Brian Portch catches it himself.

the million over there. They clean the sardines and plonk them on a big grill plate with coarse salt. I must say that, with lemon squeezed over and a bottle of white plonk on the beach, you're really into something good.

The Portches moved, while I was writing this book, from Chiswick High Street, where his shop was open in the front and they had to pull a crinkly blind down with a hook at the end of the day, when they closed the shop. There was sawdust on the floor and all sorts of people came to gaze and buy, including some very poor people who came to buy what they could afford – and there always *is* something that they can afford.

I was happy to do the opening ceremony for them of their grand new premises in Devonshire Street which is off the main drag. They also have another shop in Kingston Lane, Teddington. The opening was a colourful one, held on the pavement, with gaily coloured decorations and silver fish balloons floating serenely above the scene. The world and his wife attended and seemed to enjoy it thoroughly.

I'm so delighted with their success, because I have come to a stage when I almost couldn't live without them, and every trip to London 'We're goin' fishin' instead of just a wishin',' to Mr. Portch's! His wife Joy has provided me with the following two recipes featuring prawns and pigeons.

Sambal Prawns with Ginger

You need: 30 raw large headless prawns; 2 tablespoons sunflower oil; 3 tablespoons lemon juice; 1 medium onion, finely chopped; 3 garlic cloves, chopped and crushed; 1 inch piece fresh ginger, thinly sliced; ½ teaspoon salt; freshly ground black pepper; ½ teaspoon cumin seeds (roasted and coarsely ground); 3 small red chillies or chilli powder to taste.

Slit down the backs of the prawns and peel, leaving on just the tail tips. Remove the dark thread down the back of the prawns. Blend all other ingredients to a smooth paste in a blender or food processor. Pour over the prawns and leave to marinate for at least 2 hours. Pat the prawns dry, thread on skewers, then brush with a little oil and cook on a barbecue or under the grill for about 1 minute per side. Do not overcook. Serve with lime or lemon wedges. Serves 6.

Pigeon and Walnut Casserole

You need: 4 pigeons (oven-ready); 1 pint water; 1 large carrot, sliced; 1 celery stick, coarsely chopped; few sprigs parsley; 1 sprig fresh thyme or pinch dried; 3 shallots, chopped; 2 garlic cloves, crushed; 1 bottle red wine; 2 oz butter; ½ lb button mushrooms; ¼ lb walnut halves; 1 tablespoon bramble jelly; salt and pepper; watercress, to garnish.

Take the breast and leg off each side of the pigeon, in one piece if you can manage it. Break up the carcasses and make a stock with the water, onion, carrot, celery and parsley and thyme. Simmer for 1 hour. Strain and reserve. Reduce the wine by half.

Roast the pigeon breasts and legs for 10 minutes in a hot oven Gas Mark 7/425°F/220°C. Meanwhile cook the shallots and garlic in 1 oz of the butter in a heavy casserole until golden. Add the pigeons, stock and wine and cook in a moderate oven at Gas Mark 4/350°F/180°C for 25 minutes. Toss the whole mushrooms quickly in the remaining 1 oz butter and add to the casserole after 10 minutes. Just before the end of cooking time add the walnuts.

Remove the pigeons from the casserole and check the sauce for seasoning. You may need to reduce it a little and if it seems to need a little more depth add the bramble jelly, a little at a time. Serve garnished with watercress. Seves 4.

PORN ALLEY AND BERWICK STREET MARKET

I think one of my favourite places in the world is Berwick Street Market, and that's why I always long to be engaged at the Globe Theatre in something or other, because I have a little plan there of leaving my handbag with the stage door keeper Brendan or his wife Beattie while I just take

Jim, my friend the Chicken Man.

a lot of polythene carriers up the market and have a little fling. The Rupert Street part of the market is the very expensive part, but if you want something very unusual, like fresh horseradish or fresh herbs of any kind, you can find them all there. You can always see the first raspberries of the season on the end barrow on the left-hand side. Of course I know everyone and going through the market is always like a sort of homecoming. The fruit there is quite remarkable and must travel a long distance to get to where we find it. That goes for the vegetables too. Even if you're not buying, but just looking at the barrows, I think it's a sight for sore eyes.

Then, of course, you come to Porn Alley: I always call it that, because all the sex shops are there. It was rather unfortunate for me, because I always wanted to have a look in the sex shops, but the minute I pressed my nose against the window the man used to come out of whichever shop it was and say, 'Hello, Beryl, how are you then? All right?' and of course I had to walk right on, so I never got a good look at any of the implements that were used in this occupation and I was very disappointed. I couldn't even send anybody on my behalf, because I don't think they would have been able to describe the gadgets or whatever adequately!

There is a beautiful shop there that sells every kind of wickerwork baskets and a lot of Chinese basketwork. It's a wonderful shop, because I'm crazy about baskets. The trouble is the handle usually goes, because the fibre they're woven from is usually rather soft. The one my friends from Yorkshire brought me back from Agadir, has unfortunately lost its bottom, because that's another vulnerable spot on these baskets. I was doing a show in Yorkshire recently and I'd got bronchitis and was really quite ill, so Millie, who was looking after me was carrying my basket for me. When I inadvertently reached rather grandly into the part of the basket where the bottom had come away from the top to take out a tissue to blow my nose, she said, 'I would have thought that somebody like you, in your position, could afford something a bit better than this!' I didn't dare go back again to finish the film until I'd bought another basket for Millie!

After having shaken the dust of Porn Alley from your heels – brogues, if you're Sister George – and resisted the porn shops and been resisted by them, and fought back the impulse to buy yet another basket, you then get into the much cheaper end of the market, which is a delight. This is where you can buy five lemons for twenty-pence, they're usually so expensive and I use so many of them, that I buy them in bundles there. I was going to get a box of them, until I realized that I couldn't possibly use a box of lemons, because they would have got soft before I'd got to the end of them. Everything is about a quarter of the price that you can pay anywhere else. I have known most of the barrow minders for years and years, because every time I've played Shaftesbury Avenue it's been my favourite haunt, and they all shout to me, 'Hello, Beryl, is Terry Wogan a pouf?' and I say, 'No' and all that sort of thing, but we always have a little chat and a laugh as I pick my way through the middle of the Market.

There are some stalls that quite baffle me which sell all sorts of funny bits of toys and monkeys that bounce on the end of elastic and sweets and chocolates that I never quite understand, because they haven't got a great big message for me. But all the vegetable stalls speak to me most enticingly, and the chicken man – the chicken man is *wonderful*! I've never tasted present day chickens like he sells. I've even got his home telephone number, so that, if I do want anything I can ring up and say, 'Look here, Jim, are you going to have that ready for me?' and if I'm not working in London, Betty, my Minder, who always looks after me when I'm in the theatre in the West End, will go along and collect it for me.

The Chinese people buy chicken wings by the gross and I've never found out what they cook with them, because there's very little meat on a chicken wing. Hattie Jacques did have a recipe for chicken wings, but she didn't live to tell it me; she was always going to, but she never did. He sells beautiful turkey drumsticks, ducks, rabbits and lots of other things and he's such a nice man. We've been friends for so many years, so I can never walk past his stall. Some days he's not there, and his stall is replaced by a cheese stall; I don't know the young men who run that, because they're comparative newcomers, but their cheeses look marvellous and are another thing I enjoy browsing over.

When I was at the chicken stall once, at the time I was doing the 'Favourite Things' television for Roy Plomley I got into the queue for the stall and a very dark man said, 'Oh, no, please go in front of me.' 'No, no', I replied, 'You see I just want to look as if I'm in the queue'. Then somebody came up and cried out, 'Oh, Hello, Beryl' and my dark friend said, 'I'm awfully sorry, I didn't recognize you. You see I'm Spanish and I didn't recognize your voice, as I've only seen your films in Spanish!' What I'm like dubbed into Spanish I dread to think, but anyway, he was quite happy to be standing in the queue next to me, so it couldn't have been too dreadful.

When you go further along the market you come to the two brothers who run flower stalls; one has a stall at the cheap end, the other is at the expensive end, but all the flowers are exactly the same price which ever end you buy them. Anyway, they're both awfully nice chaps, and the flowers are a joy to behold. Incidentally, when I recently did a trip on the Concorde to Cairo, by way of a little treat before starting this book, I was wearing a straw hat I bought all of five years ago in Berwick Street Market.

LIFE AT LANGAN'S

When I had the pleasure of meeting Michael Caine again at the premiere of his latest film 'The Whistle Blower', in which I thought he was, as always, really excellent, we had a photo taken together. He reminded me that we once did a cookery programme together on the radio. Of course 'I Remember it Well' – and it's not as strange as some people might think, because Michael is an important part of the management of one of the most famous restaurants in London, Langan's in Stratton Street, where I have been taken to dine from time to time. Although I enjoy the food there so much, my own personal choice is Langan's Bistro, which I believe was opened first and is really quite enchanting. Every now and then I go to the Edward VII Hospital to have hydrotherapy, and I always book a table at Langan's Bistro, as it's so close to the Hospital.

The Bistro really do what I call 'Painting with Food', because I believe the look and presentation of meals plays such a large part in one's enjoyment of them. It isn't 'Nouvelle Cuisine' (which I'm not actually in favour of) but they do make everything look very beautiful. The dishes are unusual and they're very clearly written out, so you know what's going to go in them. It is quite expensive for what it is, but they're delightful people, and you can get a bottle of house wine which is very unintoxicating, very mild sort of wine. Each time I've been, I've taken Rick my driver, who has driven me there, because there's nowhere to park and with his taxi sign up I think you can park practically anywhere. Betty Robertson-Milne, my dresser lives quite near (only two bus stops away) and she picks me up after I've been in the baths and had my hydrotherapy and we go to Langan's Bistro, which opens at half past twelve. Usually my appointment with my dishy doctor is at half past one or two, so I always book the table and they have something quick and easy and fabulous for us to eat. It's all so tempting and I really think that it is the best English restaurant that I've come across, except for the most beautiful hotel I stayed in when I was making the film 'Joseph Andrews', the Lord of the Manor at Upper Slaughter.

WIGS AND CORSETS AT UPPER SLAUGHTER

We had a month in Bath and it was that frightfully hot summer we had in 1976. I remember saying to Peggy Ashcroft on the way home, 'Oh, I'm not going to bother to take my wig off' (I'd got my corset off and slipped into 'something loose', as we say). 'Oh, Peggy, this is really row weather,' I told her. 'I don't actually know what you mean,' she replied. Just at that moment we turned the corner and there was a man having a steaming row, with every obscene word that you could think of – but he was quite by himself. 'That's actually what I meant, Peggy,' I said. 'He's having a row with himself!'

The people at the Lord of the Manor Hotel fed me as if I was a princess. I wasn't in all day (we ate on location from a van that came round) but every night when I came home there was a little drink waiting for me on the corner of the bar. 'Oh, Hello, I'm in,' I would say when I arrived home exhausted from those terrible wooden period corsets we wore for the film in all that heat. 'Now, take that drink up to your bedroom,' they would say. If I hadn't phoned down within an hour for a meal they would ring me up and say, 'Are you all right? What would you like in your room?' After a day's filming I didn't feel that I could sit in a restaurant after wearing hideous make-up all day and having had it cleaned off by the make-up artists. So I used to stay upstairs and learn the words for the next day. They would recite all kinds of things to me over the phone, like Quail with Savoury Sauce, Roast Beef or Savoury Pancake – they'd run through their whole dinner menu for me and I used to pick what I wanted and it would be delivered straight, as soon as it could be cooked, to my bedroom. I must say I was very happy with them and they had a huge black cat, named Lord of the Manor, after the Hotel – or perhaps it was the other way around. Anyway he and I were bosom buddies.

THE TERRAZZA

An entirely different sort of restaurant is, in fact, very close to where I live, and nobody knowing Ashford in Middlesex would believe there was such a grand Italian Restaurant in the vicinity. It is called The Terrazza and I have taken all sorts of people there. Roy Plomley; Siân Phillips and her husband Robin Sachs; and everybody from my publishers. It's quite unbelievable: they are the friendliest people I know. When I go in it's great

big hugs and kisses and there are always flowers on the table, which they give me to take home afterwards in a little arrangement, which is a beautiful touch. When I had written my first two books, *So Much Love* and *The Cat's Whiskers* the books were at the table, waiting for me to sign. That's lovely, isn't it?

They bring a trolley first of all to explain all the hors d'oeuvres that you can possibly imagine, and if you ask for any alternatives the waiter, says, 'But of course we have!' and you get another list, which he reels off, like fresh asparagus and on and on. Then another trolley comes along with all the fish – all the food that you could ever eat: 'We have guinea fowl, we have King Prawns on a skewer, scallops cooked in garlic butter, and then lobster' (that's one of the hors d'oeuvres, little lobsters).

Sometimes in restaurants you feel they're trying to push you out and they're in a hurry: sometimes you don't want to be in a hurry – you only have a few snatched moments with an elusive friend, and you have to talk, because there's so much to say. At the Terrazza they never hurry you. There is a restaurant in Maiden Lane that is quite famous, and if I've been there after a show, which I must say I do very, very seldom, all the chairs are on top of the tables and you feel rather like 'Monsieur Hulot's Holiday', because they really are pushing you out; they don't want to stay any longer (mind you, some of the waiters are rather elderly).

The Terrazza at Ashford is quite the opposite: they do a roaring trade at lunch time and in the evening. I think at lunch time it's mostly expense account Charlies, because it is by no means inexpensive, but for the friendliness and the courtesy and the feeling of really being made welcome it is outstanding, and the food surpasses even that. If you order any of the fresh fish, they will cook it. You can have sea bass, salmon, crab and those beautiful fresh Mediterranean prawns in their rare form of grey, before they turn pink after being boiled for only two minutes with dill. The only time I've ever seen that before was in California, where you can pick the dill from the side of the road.

The food is wonderful and they cook all the Italian cakes. You have your Italian meringue, your Italian trifle, and they insist on sticking strawberries or raspberries on to everything, whether you want it or not, if you're having pudding.

Sometimes I don't succeed in eating all the food, which, is indeed a challenge, because there is a great deal of it. (I think they hope I'm going to live up to the Italian saying 'May your shadow never grow less'). If I can't eat everything, they make a beautiful thing like a swan, which is a catty

97

bag (or a doggy bag if you have a dog) and they put the food you haven't quite been able to manage yourself into tinfoil twisted into this graceful swanlike shape for you to take it home to your four-legged friends. This is just one more present and one more lovely touch.

ELENA

I was talking earlier of Elena whom I've known for years and years and who is now to be found at L'Escargot in Greek Street, which really is frightfully swish. I love going there because of Elena, and if anybody suggests an expensive lunch that's where I would take them. The food there has totally changed, it's now really 'Nouvelle Cuisine'. Sometimes if I'm very nervous I don't really want to eat very much at all, but I don't see how great big hulking men – and men *do* eat a lot of food – go there and come out satisfied. I suppose Elena sees that they have enough to eat.

A starter there might be an artichoke heart with a little bit of dressing on, a few pretty green leaves with a spray of redcurrants laid across it. It looks most artistic, but you're through it in three minutes flat. The food though, is beautifully cooked, and they have the most unique combinations of food. I always ask Elena, 'Well, what do you think I would like today, Elena?' and she always gives me her very best advice, and everbody comes out feeling absolutely delighted with what they've had and delighted with Elena. She amazes me, because she's a great grandmother now, and I believe is writing a book. She's such a splendid person, with the real Italian quality. She has always been so kind and so wonderful to me and I hope she has a great success with the book – I'm sure she will, because she's made the restaurant a great success.

DECIPHERING TASTES

When I do go to restaurants, which is not often, and I'm given something I don't know about, I try and decipher as I'm eating it what they may possibly have put into it. When I was in South Africa I was defeated by something I found quite delicious and which had a very unusual taste. It was something I had in restaurants mainly, and I never won when I was out there. It was called Pickled Fish.

Still on the subject of South Africa; if you talked about corn-on-the-cob they wouldn't know what you meant, because over there they're called 'mealies' – and when you pass the mealie fields there's always a tiny little boy outside, selling these wonderful, almost white corn-on-the-cobs. You see, as soon as they go the orangey colour, they're far too tough to cook.

Mealies

Boil the mealies (the palest yellow you can find) and never put salt in the water, because that immediately makes them tough. Add the salt, and the butter or margarine, when youre eating them. Then they'll be lovely, and are definitely among my favourite things from South Africa.

Picnics were the order of the day for me in South Africa. The company were always organizing things for me to do every Sunday, so I was never left sitting in the hotel. We used to have the most wonderful picnics. Everyone was crazy about cricket and played it on every beach that we went to on a Sunday. Of course, if there was some surf they never saw me, because I was in the surf all day (some beaches have surf, some don't, depending on which ocean you're facing). They used to hollow out a pineapple or a water melon and fill it with rum and just put it by the edge of the sea to cool. By the time we'd finished the cricket match we were all exhausted and were ready for this wonderful picnic that they all seemed to magic up for me.

I couldn't do a lot towards it, because I was staying in a hotel and if you're in a hotel you're absolutely stuck, because you haven't got a refrigerator, you haven't got anything. I could buy a few bits of cheese to take to it or a bit of fruit, but that was ordinary stuff compared to what they brought. Sometimes they would cook a pie and let it cool in their fridge and bring it to the beach.

I had to find a way to repay their kindness and hospitality (the time had just slipped by when I was there, thanks to all the lovely things they dreamed up for me) so I asked John Boulter if I could give a little party at his house. He agreed that it would be wonderful, and, as he had all these servants I told you about (something I'm certainly not used to) they dug a pit and put charcoal in the bottom, and they put a sort of metal grid over the top of this pit. This was going to turn out to be a barbecue or *braavleis*, as they call it in South Africa: it means 'burning flesh', which is not a very appetising translation, I think!

I entertained about thirty people: I bought half a sheep and there were baked potatoes in tinfoil – I'd been preparing all Saturday night, because it was going to be Sunday – and I'd made salads and a very exotic fruit salad with liqueur poured over it. There were all the drinks you could possibly think of. Everybody came about two o'clock and we started with a cricket match: we had terrible names for the teams, which are probably too obscene to mention. We all played very badly and nobody minded and

99

we kept going in and having drinks and snacks etc. – there was food all the time. This was in John's huge garden and the party went on until three o'clock in the morning. There's no twilight in South Africa; it's bright sunlight, then suddenly it's very dark and the mozzies start biting you, and if you're not jolly careful and have insect repellant or hair spray (which I have put on in error) on your skin, it's going to be *mange tout*.

This day was a *great* success, and it was all done very easily. I think the whole thing, with drinks going the whole time for thirty people – and that was spirits, whisky, gin, brandy, wine (red and white) and beer cost me all of £35, so you can imagine what the prices were like in 1961.

THE ALL-ENGLISH PICNIC

I find the English attitude to picnics very hard to fathom: they're something I absolutely love, but I can never believe my eyes at what goes on when people are looking for a picnic site. It's extraordinary that if somebody pulls into a lay-by at the side of the road, every other car goes into the same lay-by. If I have a picnic I want to be totally by myself, or with whoever I'm with, but they all seem to follow each other, and, of course, if you get in first, then they all come piling in after you. The English have a sort of primus stove, a kettle and sandwiches. I think these must be the dullest things in the world to take on a picnic.

My idea of a picnic is to take one of those cold boxes that will keep the stuff you've had in the fridge very cold, otherwise it does get very slushy and sloshy. I like to have a starter with a picnic – perhaps an avocado – and have little chairs to sit on, and dish it out from the boot of the car. Then you can have it like a proper meal. If you want something like a prawn cocktail to start with I'd advise you not to put the dressing on until you serve it, but keep the prawns and the lettuce crisp in the cold box. I am in great favour of taking a cold chicken that has been, perhaps, roasted with a little tarragon on it or a cold **Steamed Chicken**:

Steamed Chicken   *Mix some Hellman's mayonnaise, salt, some lemon juice, some Lea and Perrins and a heaped teaspoon of curry powder together. Skin a steamed chicken, cut it up into pieces and put them all out nicely on a plate. Then pour the mayonnaise mixture over the chicken, put it in the fridge and let it settle. Then put some foil over the top of it before you take it out with you. Put this in the bottom of the cold basket, so make sure you got a dish that will fit.*

That can be the main course, with perhaps a little Potato Salad.

I would eat the **Steamed Chicken** or Roast Chicken with Tarragon with my fingers, and perhaps have some cold new potatoes with it, with a sprinkling of parsley on them, which are very nice to eat with cold chicken. Always have some salt with you on a picnic, wrapped in foil: it's fatal if you haven't.

Afterwards, it's either cheese or fresh fruit, a bottle of cold white wine, and if there are children with you, something like pineapple juice that you've kept very cold in the fridge and put, like the cold white wine, into a thermos flask. Pour the wine or juice in the flask, screw the top on and it will keep just as cold as it would keep anything else hot. People don't often connect thermos flasks with keeping things cold, but they are completly effective. Take a few pretty paper napkins, and there is always room for a few ordinary plates in the back of the car (I hate paper plates) and knives and forks which you put in your picnic basket. Make sure you take a bin liner to collect the bits and pieces in afterwards, so you don't leave a mess wherever you have your picnic.

Here is one good recipe for a **Picnic Pie**:

Picnic Pie

To make the pastry for a big pie (I'd halve the quantities for me) you need 12 oz flour, 4 oz lard and 4 oz of water. Rub the fat into the flour and add enough cold water to make firm pastry.

Roll this out and use it to line an 8 inch loose-bottomed tin, keeping some aside for the lid. Mix together 12 oz of shredded chicken; 12 oz of ham; 8 oz of sausagemeat; fresh herbs, if you can possibly get them and 4 whole hard-boiled eggs. Put this mixture into the pie case. Then roll out the pastry for the lid. I always put a little pie filter in my pie, a little hole in the top, to let the steam out – 'Paint' the top with yolk and the white of egg beaten up. Place in the oven at Gas Mark 6/400°F/200°C and bake it for one hour and a quarter. This is an absolute feast and will feed a great number of people.

With this you can have a watercress and radish salad, which is rather lovely, or you can have a very crisp lettuce, which you will have kept in the cool box.

9
Poor King John: Surfeits of Lampreys and Other Rare Treats

istory, like most things, goes in cycles: some kings, who used to get a bad press in history books when we were very young, now have appreciation societies dedicted to rubbing out their previous wicked image in favour of painting them whiter than white. No king ever had a worse reputation than King John. As A. A. Milne put it:

> **King John was not a good man**
> **He had his little ways,**
> **And sometimes no one spoke to him**
> **For days and days and days.**

One Victorian history book summed up his character as 'nothing but a complication of vices, equally mean and odious, ruinous to himself and destructive to his people. Cowardice, inactivity, folly, levity, licentiousness, ingratitude, treachery, tyranny and cruelty' were among the 'qualities' listed in his press notices of 1858, but by 1972 in Maurice Ashley's splendidly illustrated and remarkably detailed *Life and Times of King John*, of which Lady Antonia Fraser, or Mrs. Harold Pinter as I believe she prefers to be known, was the General Editor, we read that 'unquestionably John was an extremely maligned king' and that 'he took a thoroughly intelligent and immensely energetic interest in the running of the country'. Well, you pays your money and you takes your choice.

Certainly he seems to have been, you could say, a little careless, like when he lost the crown jewels and most of the royal treasure in the Wash during his last campaign. I mean the river Wash, of course, and actually it was his followers who, when trying to negotiate the mouth of the river found 'the ground opened in the midst of the waters and whirlpools sucked in everything, men and horses'. It's they who have my sympathy – never mind the crown jewels.

John was the first king to have to sign away a great many of his powers to the barons when they could stand his little ways no longer; as the ancient forerunner of our parliament they got together at Runnymede to make him sign Magna Carta, the start of civil liberties for the common man – women didn't get much of a look in in those days. But – *was* it Runnymede? I incline towards local legend here in Wraysbury, that the actual signing took place much nearer home for me, in King John's Close, one of his favourite haunts in which he used to console himself by quaffing the local brew, possibly rough cider with peaches, during the days and days and days when neither his Queen nor the court were speaking to him. He's supposed to haunt the Close on the first Friday of the month, and I have an idea I saw him being rowed past at twilight last August, but it might have been a trick of the light. Whoever it was had a goblet to his lips and was singing 'God rest ye merry, Gentlemen' quite loudly. All of which gives me a sneaking sympathy for the poor old boy, who was actually under fifty when he died, as some of the early history books used to say 'of a surfeit of lampreys'. Here, too, there's a lot of confusion. Lady Antonia suggests in her book that (understandably) sick and distressed by his losses in the

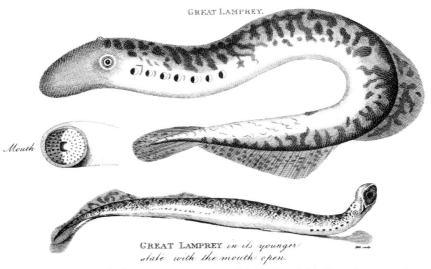

GREAT LAMPREY.

Mouth

GREAT LAMPREY *in its younger state with the mouth open.*

Not pretty and obviously poisonous. After all it did kill 2 of our royals!

Wash, he is said to have worsened his fever by supping too greedily on peaches and new cider, after which he could hardly drag himself along to the Bishop of Lincoln's Castle at Newark on the Trent – I've passed it often on my way to appear in pantomime in Leeds – where he died after three days.

Whether the lampreys did or did not play a part in all this, they certainly were prominent in historical times. Described as a 'strange sucker fish' – perhaps second cousin once removed to an eel – living in the waters of the Severn, between Worcester and my birthplace of Hereford, they were favourites of other crowned heads, including his own father Henry II, who was also said to have died of 'a surfeit of lampreys'. John's son Henry III was so little daunted by all this that he had lampreys sent every year from the Severn to wherever he was holding court. He ordered the High Sheriff of Gloucester 'to bake him all the lampreys he can get and send them by his cook. And that when he shall be nearer Severn, then to send them unbaked so long as they may come sweet, for him and his queen to eat'!

The exclamation mark is my own, on learning that these now rare fish, mainly caught and eaten by fishermen who live near the river had to be baked in a pie every year in Gloucester as part of its dues to the Crown. I wonder if the Chancellor of the Exchequer today might be interested in a particularly superlative example of Letty's Fish Pie to be despatched to him yearly Recorded Delivery in lieu of other dues from Honeypot? Even Catherine the Great commanded a great lamprey pie to be conveyed to her in Russia, which must have been something of a hazard, considering the non-existence of refrigeration and the slowness of travel at the time. Although she obviously survived she did not ask for them again, and one wonders whether perhaps she had the pie tasted first by some of her chaps at court who were no longer enjoying her favours.

Fishmongers no longer stock lampreys because parts of them are considered to be poisonous. Anyway, for the more adventurous and brave among my readers I submit, with a touch of hesitation, a recipe which Shirley Sutton of the White Swan at Twickenham, gave me from one of her library of cook books. I offer the consoling thought that, if you don't want to venture as far as the river Severn, mackerel can be substituted.

Potted Lampreys   *You need: four lamprey or mackerel; one teaspoon ground mace; one teaspoon dried tarragon; half a teaspoon turmeric; two bay leaves; six cloves; a quarter ounce of white pepper; two teaspoons salt; a quarter of a pound of shredded beef suet; a half pound of clarified butter.*

Clean the fish and remove their heads, also the fins and tails of mackerel, if you are using them. Leave on the skins, but in the case of the lampreys have the cartilage and the string on each side removed. Allow to drain for several hours. Mix the herbs, spices and salt and rub the fish all over with them. Place the fish in a stone jar or casserole, curling them round the sides of the pot, which should hold them with only about one inch to spare on top and sprinkle any herbs, spices and salt which have not adhered to the fish into the pot. Melt the suet and add the clarified butter, stirring gently. When hot pour into the fish. The fat should fill up all the spaces between the fish and cover them with half an inch to spare. When cold put into the refrigerator. When the fish is to be used, move and discard some of the butter: lift out the fish with the remaining butter and fry gently for ten minutes, or until cooked. All I can say is, if you want to risk trying this one 'Good luck' and keep me posted. Maybe stick to the mackerel!

Shakespeare in his play 'King John' suggests that the king gave orders for his young nephew Prince Arthur, whom he regarded as a threat, to be murdered, but that his jailer Hubert hadn't the heart to do it and poor Arthur was killed jumping from the castle wall after his escape. The playwright has John poisoned by a monk. It's unlikely now that we'll ever know for sure whether it was the fish, or the monk, or the scrumpy cider what, in the words of Eliza Doolittle, 'done him in', but I hope I've played my little part in pleading for a fair hearing for poor King John. After all, he *was* a neighbour, in a manner of speaking.

HANNAH AND THE PISSY PORK PIE

Five centuries on, lived one of the great cookery experts of her time, Hannah Glasse, and a book of hers, published in 1734, came into my hands in Wraysbury when I went to lunch at the Green Man. The publican and his wife, who coincidentally have the same name as mine, Reid – they are Tony and Betty – lent it to me when they heard I was writing this book. The book belonged to Tony's great-grandmother, who had put her name, C. Menzies in it in 1781. It's called *The Art of Cooking – Made plain and easy, which exceeds anything of the kind yet published* ! Well, Mrs. Glasse, the Fanny Craddock of her day, didn't suffer from false modesty. This must have been a Bestseller, even without the benefit of television, because this was a 'New Edition: Improvements, And also the order of the Bill of Fare for month, in the Manner the difhes are to be placed upon the Table, in the prefent Tafte.' No – it's not a misprint, it's the way that *sses* were written as *ffs* in the eighteenth century; in the manner that my Lady Booby in the person of my delightful and most beautiful friend Ann Margret would have written her instructions to me, as her personal maid, Mrs. Slipslop (always supposing she had known how and that I had been able to understand them) in the film that took me to the Lord of the Manor Hotel, 'Joseph Andrews'. But Lady Booby had been a strolling – more of a high-kicking player, really – before Lord Booby made an honest, but extremely roving-eyed woman of her, and Mrs. S. was a poor old broad, so maybe not a lot of notes passed between them.

Anyway, I pass on a couple of Mrs. Glasse's recipes, the way she wrote them, in case you have the will to test your brains at translating *ffs* into *sses* and old English dishes into present day mouth-waterers.

Chefhire Pork Pie

Take a loin of pork, fkin it, cut it into fteaks, feafon it with falt. nutmeg and pepper, make a good cruft, lay a layer of pork, then a large layer of pippinf, pared and cored, a little fugar, enough to fweeten the pie, then another layer of pork; put in half a pint

*Myself as Slipslop awaiting on Sir
Thomas (Peter Bull), and Joseph (Peter Firth)
on Lady Booby (Ann Margret) in 'Joseph Andrews'.*

of white wine (that's half a bottle, mind you), *lay fome butter
on the top, and clofe your pie. If your pie be large it will take
a pint of white wine* (a whole bottle, no less: I'd be tempted to
call it 'Piffy Pork Pie'!)

Mrs. G. certainly doesn't waste words telling you how to do things – it's
very much 'take it or leave it' and if you don't know how to make your
cruft, hard cheefe.

*Sweet Carrot
Pudding*

Get two penny loavef (you'd be lucky), *pare off the cruft, foak
them in a quarter of boiling milk, let it ftand till it if cold, then
grate in 2 or 3 large carrotf, then put in eight eggf well beat and
$\frac{3}{4}$ of a pound of frefh butter, melted, grate in a little nutmeg and
fweeten to your tafte. Cover your difh with puff pafte, pour in
the ingredientf and bake it an hour.*

Her oven would have been a kitchen range, of course, like my mother had.
I've resisted the impulse to pass on Mrs. Glasse's tips of how to pluck a
fowl; we'll just have to assume you know how.

WINSTON CHURCHILL

Quite by another chance stroke of good luck I was able to read the cook book kept by Winston Churchill's housekeeper – I can't say exactly when, because there is no date in the front of the book, which is like a plain black exercise book. I was a tremendous admirer of Churchill's – I think he was quite beyond compare the greatest leader we could have had in wartime. If your hopes were down in the dumps and you listened to him speaking, perhaps on the morning news, you felt really that we were going to get the better of the enemy. Some of his sayings were quiet classic – 'Some chicken, some neck!' indeed. He just inspired people during the war, including my mother and myself, by his encouragement and his utter grit to get us through the war. We knew it was going to be tough, we knew it was going to be awful, but he was an inspiration. Here's one of his house-keeper's recipes written out in her own hand – which isn't all that easy to follow!

Rum Omelette

You need: 4 eggs; 1 tablespoon caster sugar; 3 tablespoons rum; 1 oz butter; a little jam.

Beat the egg yolks with the sugar and a teaspoon of rum. Whisk the whites and lightly fold into the yolks. Melt the butter in a frying pan. Pour in the mixture and cook for a few minutes until brown underneath then put under the grill for a few minutes until brown on top. Turn out on to sugared paper. Spread with jam. Fold over and put on a warmed dish. Pour the remaining rum around and set light.

If Churchill was partial to a 'drop of this and a drop of that' in his cooking, he's in good company: none other than Betty, who, as I've told you, looks after me in the theatre and is my good friend away from it. She has given me a super and so simple recipe, for what she calls a **Christmas Jelly** or a *Festive Jelly*.

Christmas Jelly

You need one blackcurrant jelly and half a bottle of port – we're almost back to Mrs. Glasse! But Betty says it needn't be special port 'Red biddy will do!' You also need a cup of boiling water and $\frac{1}{4}$ pint double cream. You dissolve the jelly, stir in the port when the mixture has cooled – and there you are! Decorate with the whipped cream, and there you have it: nice and cheap (unless you use vintage port, which would be silly).

10
Billy Chappell and His Magic Ways

And now we come to William Chappell, or 'My darling Billy', as I like to refer to him. He has taught me practically more about anything – everything – than anybody I know. He has directed me in several revues that I've been in, on television, and the stage – most recently in 'A Little Bit On The Side', which brought back Monica, up-dated and trying to be frightfully trendy on the narcotics scene after decades at the same school, but still wearing the antediluvian gymslip and the ever-handy knickers for secreting all manner of treats, like 'Smelly Lena' and the sago pudding that reminded her of tadpoles! The 'new girl' at the school was Janet Mahoney, a delightful girl and a very talented actress, whom we don't see nearly enough of, because her husband, impressario Duncan Weldon wants to keep her to himself. I can see his point, because she's such a delight, but it's a shame, all the same.

Billy Chappell 'many talented gastronome'.

I say to Billy, 'Oh, I can't possibly do that,' and he says, 'Don't be so silly – *of course* you can!' He absolutely forces me into things, and then, of course, it all turns out to be a great success, because I never know whether I can do things or not, and if you're stretching yourself as a career person, then you really do have to listen to people who are the onlookers and so obviously know more than you.

But there his talent doesn't end. He does designs for the Royal Ballet Company for Sir Frederick Ashton, he designs costumes, he designs scenery, he's done two books about Edward Burra, one book about Margot Fonteyn. He's now, like me, having a little struggle with himself, because he's writing a book, his own autobiography, in fact, but he's much more precise than me, because I'm a sort of hashmagundy, and do it any old how. Billy has to write it all down and get it correct. He's also taught me more about cooking, perhaps, than I've learnt from anybody else. The main thing he's taught me are the short cuts: things like crême brûlée and so on were *impossible*, but not with Billy. We had such fun one Sunday talking about his 'little ways' – his magic ways, with food, that I'll try and recall it as the double act we've been so happily for so many years.

ME: Now, come on Billy; let's do something really sexy, like go through the short cuts!

BILLY: Well, what shall we start with?

ME: What about that lovely tongue I had at your house one day?

BILLY: You mean **Tongue with Madeira**? Well, that's one of the simplest of all, because it's a cheat.

ME: I love cheats! Tell us about your **Tongue with Madeira Sauce**:

Tongue with Madeira Sauce

This should *be made from a freshly home cooked tongue, but that, although rewarding, is a long and tedious business. So you just go to a delicatessen – it must be a good delicatessen, like Harrods and buy some very good,* thick *slices of tongue (you need one and a half slices per person), which you cut into halves and lay exquisitely on a dish. Then all you have to do in the way of cooking is make the Madeira Sauce.*

Have standing by ¾ pint of heated milk. Make a roux in a shallow saucepan, from 2 oz butter and 1 heaped dessertspoon flour. Add the milk little by little until you have a thickish white sauce. Remove from the heat. In a small bowl, mix 1 heaped teaspoon mustard powder, 1 heaped teaspoon caster sugar, 1 dessertspoon tomato purée and a good big dash of Worcester sauce. Blend it into a paste and stir into the white sauce. Return it to the heat and add 1 tablespoon double cream. Finally add a port–sized glass of a decent Madeira. Stir well and when the sauce is really hot, season with salt and pepper. Pour it over the tongue and place in a moderate oven at Gas Mark 4/350°F/180°C until the sauce has heated the tongue gently through. Then you offer it up, and unless people are very sharp they don't know it's not the most beautifully cooked fresh tongue in the world.

ME: What do you serve with it?

BILLY: Mashed potato of the best possible kind, with butter and a little cream and pepper and salt. Now what about Pasta?

ME: Oh, I love Pasta.

BILLY: Well, that's a very quick easy thing, isn't it?

ME: Yes, but sometimes it tastes dreary.

BILLY: Well, in the ordinary way it's quick and easy, but if you've got to make a fresh and really delicious tomato sauce it's quite a business. If you do tagliatelli, you just cook it and it literally takes about fifteen minutes.

ME: You mean the green tagliatelli?

It's impossible to be unhappy with the lovely view from my dining room.

BILLY: I prefer the plain tagliatelli – the white one.

ME: In narrow strips?

BILLY: Yes. The flat ribbon kind. For **Creamed Tagliatelli with Cheese**:

Creamed Tagliatelli with Cheese

You just put a lump of butter with the tagliatelli, after cooking for about 15 minutes, until it's soft but not too limp, and pour 1 tablespoon cream over it, then, if you're very rich you grate some fresh Parmesan – but only if you're very rich, because Parmesan is the most incredibly horrible price. If you can't afford that, you go and buy one of those little cartons at the delicatessen or the grocer's and just shake it over. So, it's just butter, cream and Parmesan on top of the hot tagliatelli, which has been boiled with a little salt and black pepper. Use double cream, and if you want to, add some strips of sliced ham to the mixture. That's very nice, too, and almost equally quick. Just mix it in, and there you are.

Now, Beryl, I've got two cold sauces I do, which my mother taught me when I was about twelve or thirteen years old . . .

ME: You were lucky!

BILLY: To my great pleasure I found my mother's sauces in Elizabeth David's book on sauces – a special book that she wrote about sauces and those kind of things.

ME: Well, I think she's very good, but I also think that recipes do get swiped over the generations.

BILLY: Well, this has been swiped from quite a way back – I wonder where mother swiped it. Anyway the first was a Sauce you had with **Cold Boiled Beef** or Cold Boiled Gammon, or anything like that which you thought was a bit boring and you were using it up:

Sauce for Cold Meat

All it consisted of was a mixture of mustard, lemon juice, vinegar and plenty of sugar, stirred up together, and that's it – you didn't cook it or anything. You just put a dollop of it on your plate and dipped the meat into it, and it's very, very delicious with cold boiled beef or gammon.'

ME: Oh, that's rather classy!

BILLY: The other sauce was a **False Mayonnaise**, which was also in Elizabeth David's book, I discovered, years and years later. That consisted of:

False Mayonnaise   *The yolks of hard boiled eggs – a yolk per person I would think would be a very good guide, and you crush them – I know you're very fond of pestles and mortars, so you could do it that way, or else you can do it as I do, with a fork, and put in a little single cream while you're mashing it, which makes it easier to get it very smooth. Then, again, you put in plenty of salt and pepper, a lot more cream, a squeeze of lemon juice and a little bit of wine vinegar, and that's it. Make a nice smooth sauce of it and you eat that with anything in preference to salad cream.*

ME: So it's like mayonnaise?

BILLY: Well, it's a false mayonnaise, but it's much nicer than salad cream.

ME: Oh – I couldn't agree more.

BILLY: It's much nicer, because the ingredients are much fresher.

ME: When I see a salad in anybody's house and they bring out that jar, I kind of faint away.

BILLY: I know – I do, too, you feel you might have gone to Dick's cafe around the corner.

ME: Except we haven't go one here – well, not just round the corner, anyway. By the way, I've lost my pestle and mortar, so I'm going to have to make it your way, with a fork!

BILLY: Well, there we are. You were mentioning **Crème Brûlée** earlier.

ME: Yes, because you taught me how to do it.

BILLY: I know, but I've forgotten. It's so long since I've done it that I've forgotten.

ME: Well, I can remember exactly, because I've sort of dined out on it. It came in handy when I was doing Edward Albee's play 'Counting The Ways' at the National, and this married couple go on at length about it, because she has let her mind wander while she was doing it, so it got '*Burnt*' as Michael Gough said bitterly, so he'd never had his beloved **Crème Brûlée**! Your having taught me how to do it was very helpful then, because otherwise, when they go into a long explanation about it I would not have been able to correct them if it hadn't been right. I'm funny that way – kind of set in my ways, as well as Counting them!

BILLY: The thing is, in my version you don't have to have a double saucepan.

ME: Oh, I can't bear them – I wouldn't do it if it was in a double saucepan!

BILLY: I dread double saucepans – I suppose they're sensible, but I don't know.

ME: I don't know either, because I don't know what they mean. That's why I took to you. I *hate* double saucepans! My mother used to use them for making porridge, but I don't know what that was all about.

Michael Gough offering me the remains of a rose in 'Counting the Ways'.

BILLY: Well, you describe how you do **Crême Brûlée** – my way: I've forgotten.

ME: Yes – I'll 'Do It Your Way.' This is all beginning to sound exactly like Edward Albee – it's catching, really. Anyway, for **Crême Brûlée, Billy's Way**:

Crême Brûlée, Billy's Way

Take a large carton of double cream and pour it into an ovenproof dish. You put in 2 whole eggs – your original recipe was between 2–4 tablespoons sugar; actually I use two, and I find that quite sweet enough. You've pre-heated the oven at Gas Mark 4/350°F/180°C. Beat all these ingredients up together, and cook this mixture slowly, because it's going to be beautiful: you mustn't cook it till it gets really stiff, because it then gets to be just a Big Boys' Egg Custard. You must cook it till it's not quite set in the middle and that's the time to take it out, let it go cold, and then put it into the fridge. The next day, when you're going to use it, you cover the top with a very good layer of caster sugar – make sure that the sugar reaches every tiny corner of the dish that you've put it in, because otherwise it just somehow doesn't work – I don't know what it is. It must be caster sugar, but if you haven't got that but you do have a little whizzer, you put some granulated into that and it turns into caster sugar. Then you get the grill fairly hot – then with your oven gloves at the ready you put the dish under and watch it. You must never take your eyes off it, or you'll end up, like poor Michael Gough, with 'No Crême Brûlée!' This is definitely not the time to be Counting the Ways to anything! You turn it round with your oven gloves on – you must watch the colour all the time, because what you want it to be like is very fine, light brown toffee – hot brittle toffee. When you think it's done all over and it's fairly brown, then you take it out, you let it go cool and then you put it into the refrigerator until you serve it. I must say I've gone a little bit mad recently, because I allow my guests a weeny little jug of Cointreau to pour on to it. I must say that's wonderful – exotic!

BILLY: Oh, that's very, very grand; very high style.

ME: Although I dread double saucepans I have been known to make **Zabaglione**: It's that lovely, frothy sort of eggy thing that you get in Italian restaurants, with usually those super sponge fingers that you use for your 'Pushers':

Zabaglione

I would say again you need a yolk of an egg per person and you beat those up in a china bowl. Have some water simmering in a saucepan, put the china bowl over the saucepan, and add some sugar gradually to it – I would say perhaps, for four people, 2 dessertspoons and preferably caster sugar, because it mixes in so much more easily, with a wire whisk, keep whisking the egg yolks and the sugar all the time, but you mustn't let it get like scrambled eggs, because that can very easily happen. You keep the water strictly on a simmering heat. Then if you have Marsala wine (which I very seldom have) you add a couple of dessertspoonfuls or you can use a sweet dark sherry, but it's not as good – to me it's like varnish . . .

BILLY: I love dark sherry – varnish!

ME: It's like the Mayor of Somewhere who'd never tasted olives before and was offered them at a party. 'Ee,' he said, 'The cat's pissed in't plums again!' But, to get back to the **Zabaglione**.

You put the 'Varnish' or the Marsala wine into it, watching all the time that it doesn't get into a scrambled eggy thing at all – it's got to be as light as fairies and frothy and beautiful and smoothly almost liquid. Served in a wine glass with a couple of these lovely sponge fingers – it's really, I think, quite a marvellous pudding. Of course the yolk of the egg has 100% fat in it, which is a little upsetting to me. . . .'

BILLY: It's nourishing, that – light and nourishing.

ME: Light and nourishing? Righto, Billy, you do it your way! Do you often cook soup, Billy?

BILLY: Yes, I do, continually: I make a very good fresh tomato soup.

ME: Oh that's the one I had at your house, but I've never known how to make it.

BILLY: It's much easier to make your **Fresh Tomato Soup** now you can get those big tomatoes because they've got more flavour than the ordinary terrible old tomatoes that you buy in shops nowadays. You can do it with canned ones – it's not *quite* as good but perfectly all right for quickness . . ..

Fresh Tomato Soup

Take 2 large Italian-type tomatoes and chop into small pieces. Finely chop 1 onion, put it in a saucepan with the tomato and cover with a good beef stock (your butcher will give you bones). Bring to simmering point and add 1 heaped dessertspoon soft light brown sugar. Stir well. As soon as the tomato is really softened, mash the mixture thoroughly and push through a sieve to get rid of the seeds and skins. Add sufficient stock to suit your own taste in consistency. Now season well with pepper and celery salt; and 1 heaped teaspoon tomato purée to enhance the colour. Next add the juice of $\frac{1}{2}$ a lemon; a large pinch of allspice; $\frac{1}{2}$ a teaspoon of freshly grated nutmeg and a big splash of Worcester sauce. Serve hot, with croûtons, fried very crisp in vegetable oil.

ME: My dear friend and Agent, Robert Luff – 'We've been together now' like in the song, and it's more years than either of us cares to count – some years ago bought a lovely hotel in Scarborough called the Royal Hotel. It used to belong to Tommy Laughton, who was Charles Laughton's brother. I thought it lovely: it was the first really posh hotel I'd stayed at. There was a little bowl of fruit in the room and I thought I was everybody! Of course, there were no bathrooms or anything with the rooms

Robert Luff and his beautiful hotel in Scarborough.

then, which didn't worry me at all at the time, I think it would now, because you never know when you want to go, do you?

Now Robert Luff has spent I think really millions of pounds on it and they've got a modern leisure centre and solarium and jacuzzi bath and so on, and he stays there himself, because he has a lot of business to do there, apart from running all our lives.

We talked on the telephone the other day and he said, 'You know, I longed for an old-fashioned pudding, like a Bread and Butter Pudding and I suggested to the Chef' – he's got a most fabulous chef who runs one of the two restaurants in the hotel – 'that there should be a well-known old-fashioned British pudding of a different sort served every day', which seems the most marvellous idea.

Now I don't think anybody knows more about puddings than Billy, so now I'm going to hand over to him, to see what he can get out of it. Now Billy, what about if you were going to do a different one every day?

BILLY: I doubt if I'd be able to manage seven.

ME: Oh well, you might be able to manage five and at the weekend 'Let them eat cake,' or what about a nice trifle, or Betty's **Christmas Jelly**.

BILLY: Well, yes, I expect we'd manage. Now, let me see, we've got Mother's Bread and Butter Pudding, the Old-Fashioned Rice Pudding, Jam Roly Poly, Apple Charlotte, Ethel Pudding, your mother's Queen of Puddings . . .

ME: Oh, and there's **Summer Pudding**, and there, we've got it made. Oh, there's no end to it – I say, steady – we're getting quite carried away. The whole idea's quite gone to our heads!

BILLY: Yes, that sounds good if you want them to Eat Cake. **Summer Pudding**, is terribly old-fashioned: not many people make it now, but I absolutely love it, when the fruit is in season.

ME: Well here goes with my recipe:

Summer Pudding

*I'm not terribly good at cutting bread in the right shapes and sizes, so I buy that very thinly -sliced white bread. You line a bowl with this, with a piece at the bottom that fits. Prepare the equivalent of a couple of punnets of redcurrants (the topping and tailing is a bit of a fag) and cook them in a little water – I use honey, not sugar, which makes for a better flavour, I think. When they are really squashy and cooked they have a wonderfully sort of acidy smell and taste. Then I put a punnet or two of raspberries in, just to turn over with the redcurrants in the saucepan and, before I take the saucepan off the heat, I add ½ a packet of red jelly, torn into squares and let that dissolve. Now this is a bit of a cheat, but it's an awfully good idea – otherwise when you turn the **Summer Pudding** out it often collapses. Pour this into the bowl lined with the very thin white bread and then cut a lid from the bread to fit the bowl, trimming off any surplus edges so that it's just the right shape. Put the lid on, press it down with a saucer and I usually put the iron on top so that the bread is absolutely saturated with the juice from this mixture. Put it into the refrigerator and just leave it till it's set. I would, for preference, make the pudding the day before. Then you turn it out on to a plate and it's like a beautiful sort of fruit crammed bread pudding, with the bread very thin on the outside and saturated with the juice from the fruit. If people like cream it adds the final touch to a lovely old fashioned pudding, so rarely made these days – but it's a gem.*

Billy is always so inventive with what he calls his 'cheats' and his 'False this and False that' which always turn out so successfully. I was able to surprise him with a tiny 'Cheat' of my own before lunch on the day of his visit to talk about this book. As we were talking and swapping ideas for food I suddenly said, 'Do you know, Billy, there's something I can do frightfully easily – **Bombe Alaska**!:

Bombe Alaska

First turn your oven on to pre-heat at its highest setting. Again, it's a bit of a cheat, because you buy one of those sponge flans. Put it in an oven-proof dish and soak the bottom in alcohol – any kind will do. Then add fruit such as canned apricots (but not the juice, fresh raspberries, or fresh anything, or perhaps a little fruit cocktail (again minus the juice). Arrange it in the bottom of the flan case. Whisk 2 or 3 egg whites until very stiff and add 1 tablespoonful caster sugar or maybe 1½ tablespoons sugar. Put as much ice cream as you like on top of the fruit and then you cover it with the meringue mixture you've made. As with the **Crème Brûlée,** *you must make sure that it reaches every edge of the sponge, so that there are no air holes. The trick is not to leave the ice cream any space to breathe. Put it in to the very hot oven for 10 minutes exactly. Out of the oven comes the most wonderful Bombe Alaska, which stuns everybody. They always think you're awfully clever, but it's not clever at all. You've got meringue on the top which is pale brown, the ice cream which is still hard, and then you come to the fruit layer, and you can cut it in lovely big chunks. I believe it's a real luxury – almost a party thing and people can't believe you've done it yourself. Believe me, it's awfully easy.*

When Billy and Eric had lunch when they came here to talk about this book I magicked it up, really, because I hadn't got time for anything else. I started with Cold Consommé out of a can, alas, but Crosse and Blackwell's is the only one which goes solid in the tin when you leave it in the fridge. If you have consommé and it doesn't go solid, heat it and add some gelatine to it and it will go solid when it gets cold, but you have to do that the night before. On the top of the 'jelly soup', as a young friend of mine, aged five, used to call it, I poured some soured cream, then some chopped chives, and because I hadn't got any of the 'poor man's caviar' I did a little cross of anchovies, one per person on top of it, on each of our plates, and that seemed to go down a treat.

Then we had a little **Fillet of Beef** that I got from my farm butcher:

Fillet of Beef

I suppose it weighed about 2¼ lb. I prepared a little mixture of crushed garlic, dried mixed herbs, salt and pepper – ground black pepper. I'd mixed it all together and rolled the fillet of beef in it. I cooked it for 15 minutes in the hottest oven I could possibly get, then I turned it down to Gas Mark 3/325°F/170°C and cooked it for another 15 minutes. If you like beef with a pink middle, this is unbelievably beautiful: actually I was talking on the phone and I overdid it a bit – it had gone a bit grey in the middle and that was entirely my fault.

I'd cooked a few Jersey potatoes – very few, because they were very expensive at this time. The thing to do is to put some mint in when the water starts to boil and to get the full flavour out of the mint rub the leaves together – what I call scrunch it up in your hand.

I made a May Salad, because this was when we were planning to start the recording and writing of *Beryl, Food and Friends*, so called because in my mind's eye they fit together and complement one another. Into the salad went, of course, a bit of torn-up lettuce, raisins that I'd soaked overnight, chopped spring onions, very finely chopped tomatoes (without the seeds) and cucumber, which I sliced first, then cut into little squares. What I meant to put in, which was going to make me the best person in the world, was a lot of chopped walnuts, but there was so much talking and laughter that the walnuts are still sitting on the side of my draining board, awaiting their finest hour. I just forgot to do them, like the radishes, which were sitting there looking terribly pretty in the fridge. If the radishes are not hollow in the middle I love the flavour of them, when they have that hot taste. On the salad I put a French dressing; unfortunately I'd run out of 'Old Red Wine', so I had to make do with white wine, which wasn't nearly as tasty as it should have been.

For pudding I'd hollowed out three halves of 2 melons, because there were three of us and it turned out as rather a scrumptious **Melon Surprise**.

Melon Surprise

I chopped some strawberries and put them in the melon halves. Then I cut the stones out of some black cherries and put one at each corner of the strawberry mixture and I also had a Kiwi fruit, and the green of the Kiwi looked terribly pretty with it, between the black cherries with a little dump of Kiwi in the middle. I put honey on it and a little Cointreau – and it wasn't half bad, though I do say so myself.

I am told by Eric that the lunch was really worth cycling the round trip of thirty miles from Reading. I take this as a compliment, though he *is* fairly eccentric!

I'll end Billy Chappell's Magic Ways with a fairly magic starter which he passed on to me and which remains one of my top favourite starters, when Beef Tomatoes are in season. They are those lovely big tomatoes with a really appealing flavour, and here's how **Stuffed Tomatoes** get that way:

Stuffed Tomatoes

You buy as many Beef Tomatoes as you have people coming and you get a lot of the pulp out, having sliced off the top of the tomato and laid it aside for later. Discard the seeds, which I don't think are of much value. Put the pulp into a bowl, and open a can of unsweetened grapefruit segments and drain them. You may not use all the grapefruit for the recipe, but the juice is quite good to drink and you can use up any of the leftover segments afterwards, maybe grilled with a little sherry and brown sugar, as a little starter, or a pudding for yourself. Cut up as many of the segments as will measure up to equal portions with the tomato pulp and the other ingredients you're going to use, which can be a tiny can of tuna fish, some chopped anchovies and a little finely chopped onion. Mix them all together. Then for laziness you take some of that oh-so-useful standby, Hellman's mayonnaise. To this you add some salt, anchovy essence, a tiny bit of tomato purée, for colouring, and lemon juice. Mix this mayonnaise dressing in the bowl with the stuffing before you put it into the tomatoes. Then put back the top of the tomato lids which you've been clever enough to lay safely aside in the beginning of the operation. Add a little decoration of anything that's green and pretty on the top, like fennel, mint or parsley or perhaps watercress, and it makes a really unusual and beautiful starter, because it rather cleans your palate. A delicate curtain-raiser to the main theme.

11
Painting with Food – or Afterthoughts and Conclusions

*L*ooking back on the whole world of food certain conclusions have sprung to mind, among them what, to me, is the most important factor of the *look* of what you prepare for others or what is set before you. It's not going too far, I think, to say that the presentation can make or mar even the most potentially tasty meal. I think of presentation as painting with food – the hues and the tones should complement one another, as they do in the best paintings, or the contrasts should be so striking they tell their own story.

Once I was invited to a special dinner party, and I was absolutely filled with excitement. In the end it turned out not to be the happiest occasion of all. This lady, who was a renowned cook, had phoned her fortune teller or soothsayer or whatever you call them in the morning and had been told it was going to be a beautiful evening. Well, she was wrong. It started off not badly: thank God I had a long black woollen dress with black ribbon sewn roundways all the way up the dress: it was a very pretty dress with a low neck with a collar and a little black ribbon bow hanging down, but it had short sleeves. It was made by Anne Venus, who really kept me better dressed than anybody else: she had a dress shop in Birmingham, and we were great friends. Unfortunately she was killed in a road accident on black ice at a tragically young age.

I thought how glad I was that I had a woollen dress on: we were all seated in the garden at long trestle tables and we were on wooden benches. I believe – but I'm not sure – that a great many people had paid to come and I was one of the invited, so-called stars. Of course everybody was terribly pleased to be there and looking forward to the food and everything. The thing that upset me perhaps more than the drizzle and the bitter cold of the night was the fact that the food seemed to be suffering from pernicious anaemia: there were about eight courses, all exactly the same colour. They all had cream in, so they all looked white. For colour contrast you had the guests – mostly blue with the cold, with the odd red nose for variety. As the drizzle persisted were were told 'Horse blankets are available on rails in the cloakroom', and if we wanted a horse blanket we had to go and get it. My hair, which had looked kind of all right when I set out – it was what my mother would have called 'half-way decent' – and really quite pretty, began to hang down in festoons, as though it had been left out all night, as indeed it almost had.

I think those of the guests who survived the night must have died the next day of pneumonia from the cold and wet. I have never found out, because as soon as I could get him, my driver came for me and I beat it.

This was a very huge dinner party – more like a convention – and everybody was absolutely frozen, but this was not as upsetting as all the dishes looking exactly the same colour. What I like about food is that when you are cooking it, the great thing is to make it completely irresistible: the decoration of the food and the colours in the food all go to make up the art of what I call painting with food. If the dish is a pale colour, then

Now you see it . . . . . .
                    Now you don't.

it must have some sort of bright green or red decoration, or anything that is available. I even suggest using the little leaves off celery, parsley, watercress or fennel leaves or sliced red, yellow or green peppers arranged in such a way that the dish really enchants the eye, and you can't wait to get knives or forks or whatever into the food that's served you.

I think the beauty of the food is what entices people to eat. It isn't a trick, it's just more artistic if the table and the food, and, if possible, the glasses look lovely and so everything looks much more tempting to eat.

Some cookery books attract me very much: Marguerite Patten has done many lovely books and Robert Carrier's books are an absolute joy to look at. Sometimes I find Carrier's recipes a little difficult to follow, but then, he's a genius – I'm not. There are so many cookery books, all with their special qualities and I admire the authors for commiting their love of the arts of food to the written page.

Lack of perception, taste and tact among the famous are not confined to cookery experts. When I did the television programme 'Through The Keyhole' recently, I had to be invisible in the bedroom, sketching in a face from memory, as the point was to guess whose house it was. It was just before I started on the second of the 'Adrian Mole' series and I was going to go round to Chris, my friend who helps me here, to have a look at the first lot on her video, which I'd not been able to see, because I was in the theatre. I could hear the presenter, who is from Boston, drawling, 'Oh – this is obviously a *very* old-fashioned kitchen – no 'Nouvelle Cuisine' here, and obviously whoever owns this house has a very bad memory, because several of the herbs and spices have been repeated!' You can imagine how furious I was. I thought how stupid it was to say that the herbs and things had been repeated, because, of course, if you're driving up the M1 and you're going to cook the chicken with the dried mint and the lemon juice and the rest of it, would you remember exactly what *you've* got in the cupboard? I certainly can't because when I've just done something like a play or a part in a film, and you really can't remember everything that's in the pantry. I do commit a certain amount to paper, but I don't know exactly what I'm going to eat when I get back, or what I'm going to feel like – and *in case* you haven't got the dried mint, (and in the winter there's no mint growing in the garden), you naturally buy a dried herb to go with whatever you're having. So I thought he was a bit of a nana!

When we got to Yorkshire to do the programme, with David Frost as the Chairman, and Lord Lichfield, who actually guessed it was my house, there was another young man on the panel who is terribly famous and on practically everything you can think of. He was terribly rude about me. He droned on saying 'Oh, how awful – a house full of cats, and hairs on the beds – ugh. It's obviously somebody who's *never* been married, a *spinster* . . .' So I was 'Spinster of this Parish' again! Having had two marriages and a number of Gentlemen Callers, I don't think I qualify to be called a spinster. I like men and will continue to do so until the day I get carried out in a box (as I pointed out on the programme, when I was allowed to confront the panel). I couldn't, for obvious reasons, meet them in the hospitality room beforehand, and I never go afterwards, because I'm either going home or I'm going to go back to my hotel to try to reassess what I did and have what Noel Coward called 'A Little Something on a Tray' in bed.

My book is really dedicated to my friends, a great number of whom love cooking, because, funnily enough it's a great relaxation to cook if you have a day off, if you're working in the theatre or in films. It's not nearly so much fun if you have to do it every day – I appreciate that. If you do enjoy it and you get pleasure out of eating it, long may you continue to do so. Even if you only like eating, eat the best and the most attractive things you can find.

Bon appetit – and love!

Index

FOOD AND DRINK

PHOTOGRAPHS